proclamation 2

Aids for Interpreting the Lessons of the Church Year

epiphany

Richard I. Pervo and William J. Carl III

series c

editors: Elizabeth Achtemeier · Gerhard Krodel · Charles P. Price

FORTRESS PRESS   PHILADELPHIA

COPYRIGHT © 1979 BY FORTRESS PRESS

Second printing 1982

Library of Congress Cataloging in Publication Data (Revised)

Main entry under title:

Proclamation 2.

Consists of 24 volumes in 3 series designated A, B, and C which correspond to the cycles of the three year lectionary plus 4 volumes covering the lesser festivals. Each series contains 8 basic volumes with the following titles: Advent-Christmas, Epiphany, Lent, Holy Week, Easter, Pentecost 1, Pentecost 2, and Pentecost 3.
    CONTENTS: [etc.]—Series C: [1] Fuller, R. H. Advent-Christmas. [2] Pervo, R. I. and Carl III, W. J. Epiphany.—Thulin, R. L. et al. The lesser festivals. 4 v.
    1. Bible—Homiletical use. 2. Bible—Liturgical lessons, English.
[BS534.5.P76]   251   79-7377
ISBN 0-8006-4079-9 (ser. C, v. 1)

270J82   Printed in the United States of America   1–4085

Contents

Editor's Foreword

In distinction to Christmas, which originated in the West during the fourth century, the festival of the Epiphany had its origin in the Eastern church. Our earliest known reference to the Epiphany points us to late second-century Egypt as the probable time and place of its origin. We hear through Clement of Alexandria that the Gnostic sect of Basilides celebrated the Birth and Baptism of Jesus on January 5–6. In passing, we may note that in the night of January 5–6 pagan Egypt celebrated the birth of the god Aion, brought forth by the virgin goddess Kore. It is probable that the birth of that god and the waters of the Nile were related in some way. It is certain that the Christian Epiphany festival had at its beginning a twin focus, the Birth and Baptism of Jesus. In the Eastern church this festival became, together with Easter and Pentecost, one of the three major festivals of the church.

This twin focus was dissolved when beginning with the last decades of the fourth century the birth of Jesus was celebrated on December 25 also in the Eastern church. (Only the Armenian church retained January 6 as the date for celebrating Christ's Birth until the present.) With the removal of the Incarnation and Birth of Jesus from the Epiphany festival, the festival of the Epiphany required new emphases. In addition to the Baptism of Jesus, we find as chief subjects the miraculous guidance of the wise men from the East, the miracle of Cana, and other miraculous manifestations of God in Christ.

The period between the festival of the Epiphany and the First Sunday in Lent varies greatly in length depending on the date of Easter, which can fall as early as March 22 and as late as April 25. Hence the Epiphany season is at times shortened by one to five Sundays. Among Lutherans it became customary to keep the festival of the Transfiguration of Our Lord on the Last Sunday after the Epiphany.

This season draws the church's attention to the Epiphany, the manifestation or revelation of God in Christ to Jews and Gentiles. Hence the interpreter of the following pericopes should ask first of all what does God reveal, do, in this text? What does this reveal about God's presence and reality? Secondly, we might ask who is the Christ whose Epiphany is to be proclaimed and celebrated? What does the text say about him? And thirdly, we might inquire to whom does God in Christ reveal himself? What is he doing to them and for them and how does he enter their lives?

The new lectionaries used by various denominations in the United States exhibit uniformity to a large extent. Where they differ, we have usually preferred the longer texts (e.g., the Second Lesson for the Epiphany where the Episcopalians have Ephesians 3:1–12, while the Lutherans have Ephesians 3:2–12, the Roman Catholics Ephesians 3:2–3, 5–6, and the Presbyterians Ephesians 3:1–6), or else we followed the majority principle. Some lessons of a particular lectionary which had to be omitted will make their reappearance at some later point within one of the three cycles.

Richard I. Pervo is the volume's exegete. He studied at Concordia College (B.A.), Episcopal Theological School (B.D.), and Harvard University (Th.D.) and is currently Associate Professor of New Testament and Patristics at Seabury-Western Theological Seminary in Evanston, Illinois. William J. Carl III, the homiletician, is Assistant Professor of Homiletics and Worship and Instructor of New Testament Greek at Union Theological Seminary in Virginia. He is a graduate of University of Tulsa (B.S.), Louisville Presbyterian Theological Seminary (M.Div.), and University of Pittsburgh (Ph.D.)

Gettysburg, Pa.   GERHARD KRODEL

The Epiphany of Our Lord

Lutheran	Roman Catholic	Episcopal	Pres/UCC/Chr	Meth/COCU
Isa. 60:1–6	Isa. 60:1–6	Isa. 60:1–6, 9	Isa. 60:1–6	Isa. 60:1–6
Eph. 3:2–12	Eph. 3:2–3, 5–6	Eph. 3:1–12	Eph. 3:1–6	Eph. 3:1–12
Matt. 2:1–12	Matt. 2:1–12	Matt. 2:1–12	Matt. 2:1–12	Matt. 2:1–12

EXEGESIS

First Lesson: Isa. 60:1–6. This passage is part of a collection of oracles written during the early postexilic period. They express, in images that continue to exert power, the coming salvation of God. Light was one of the features of a theophany, or divine appearance. It is used metaphorically here to set forth a new understanding of salvation. The image of light makes a neat liturgical *inclusio*, or bracket, with the final Sunday of this season, which celebrates the Transfiguration of Christ.

The original setting of this pericope was in the period following King Cyrus of Persia's decree permitting the exiles of Judah to return (538 B.C.). From vv. 4–5 it is clear that this process had only begun and that it had not led to a revitalization of the land and the people. The language and ideas of Deutero-Isaiah form the background for this later prophet, who reinterprets them for a changed situation. Chap. 60 is a unified poem. The first nine verses are its introduction and initial section. The oracle is addressed to Zion and relates the movement of her native people back to Jerusalem and the coming of foreign wealth to glorify God in the cult. Deutero-Isaiah's thought is reworked because the prophet no longer looks for salvation within the normal course of historical events. It will come miraculously. To achieve this transformation the event of salvation is described as an appearance of God in the form of light. The ultimate background for this was the manifestation of a sky-god in a thunderstorm, with the signs of fire, smoke, thunder, and quaking (Ps. 18:7–15; Judg. 5:4–5, etc.), but light here stands for both the essence of deity (glory) and the divine gift (salvation). Thus the appearance of God is likened to

the rising of a star (cf. Matt. 2:2ff.) and Jerusalem to a slowly grow-
ing beacon in a world of darkness. By use of this imagery the prophet
was able to transpose the theme of salvation from the sphere of
worldly events into the realm of the supernatural. This shift is a
presupposition to much NT thought.

Second Lesson: Eph. 3:1–12. The significance of the pseudo-
nymity of Ephesians for the expositor is that Ephesians must be
allowed to speak for itself rather than be forced into the framework
of Pauline thought provided by the genuine letters. The writer seeks
to defend Paul's reputation by various means, including appeals for
sympathy based upon Paul's experience of suffering (3:1, 8, and 13).
As a reinterpretation of Pauline thought to meet new circumstances,
Ephesians is representative of one aspect of the Pauline heritage. Like
Colossians, to which it is closely related, Ephesians makes use of
speculative thought in the tradition of Jewish wisdom. This orientation
is responsible for the rather esoteric quality of the language.

Within the context of the document, 3:1–13 stands as something
of an independent unit, as the completion of 3:1 in 3:14 signifies.
For the liturgical context the leading idea of this passage is that of
the Gentile mission. All persons will be gathered together in Christ.
This gathering is interpreted cosmically rather than sociologically.
By giving the Gentile Christians a divine sanction the writer makes
ecclesiology an extension of Christology and the church a supernatural phenomenon.

Paul saw the estrangement of humanity from God as a radical gulf
bridged by Christ. The writer of Ephesians locates this alienation in
the separation of Jews from Gentiles. Reconciliation of differences
among peoples thus becomes the ultimate surprise of the divine plan
(vv. 3, 4). The agent of this reconciliation is the church (vv. 3, 10).
Thus the incorporation of Gentiles into the people of God can be
described as the decisive turning point in history, the moment when
the "hidden" becomes "revealed" (v. 6). By couching this thesis in
cosmic language the writer hoped to make it both attractive and
acceptable to his readers. His interests were centered on concrete
realities rather than heavenly mysteries. His message was, in effect,
"If you wish to see a real heavenly miracle, consider the presence of
Gentiles in the church." The Epiphany of Christ is, according to
Ephesians, an earthly explosion and not a cosmic happening alone.

Gospel: Matt. 2:1–12. The delightful legend of the magi explains
the Christian mystery to Jewish and Gentile readers in the form of a

story. There is no intrinsic connection between the stories in Matthew 1 and Matthew 2—nor, of course, between the infancy narratives of Matthew and Luke. Matt. 2:1–23 contains two separate stories brought together in a related sequence. Scripture is important for this episode, both as a source for the account and in the emphasis upon fulfillment of prophecy.

The episode of the star and its oriental interpreters parallels the story of Balaam (Num. 22—24). The tyrannical King Herod owes part of his character to the Balaam narrative and part to the wicked pharaoh who sought to slay Moses (Exod. 1). Through combination of an unusual rendition of Mic. 5:2 with 2 Sam. 5:2b in v. 6, the place of birth at Bethlehem is viewed as a fulfillment of prophetic words regarding the Messiah. V. 11 points to an implicit fulfillment of Isa. 60:6 and Ps. 72:10–11. For the evangelist such proofs were more than a literary exercise.

In this account the magi are not presented as frauds or magicians, as is the case in Acts 8:9ff. and 13:6ff. For Matthew they possess all their exotic glamour. Since they represent both the apex of scientific achievement (astrology) and the powerful attraction of oriental wisdom in a single package, it is difficult to find a modern term to translate *magi*. The appeal of acupuncture in the late 1960s and early 1970s is something of an analogy. Through practice of their profession they recognized the significance of the portent. There was nothing ordinary about this star, for it served not only as a sign but also as something of a guide, pausing for a stopover in Jerusalem and leading them on to Bethlehem. From the odd behavior of the star we can observe that the evangelist interpolated the events in Jerusalem into the story of the magi as a means for laying the groundwork of Herod's subsequent slaughter in 2:16–18.

For Matthew, too, the revelation of Christ to the Gentiles was a supernatural event accompanied by cosmic phenomena. Jesus, the King of the Jews, was honored by Gentiles, thus presaging his role as universal Savior. The form of his material dictated that Matthew present this as a story rather than as an image (Third Isaiah) or as theological speculation (Ephesians).

Herod's reaction to the infant king was that of a jealous rival. For us this is a reminder that although the kingship of Jesus is not worldly, it does threaten the rulers of this earth, for in it the inadequacy of their claims and the fraudulence of their promises to satisfy all human needs are laid bare and brought to light.

There are also reminders in this Gospel that despite the joy surrounding the Nativity and the Epiphany, Jesus will not enjoy life at ease in a palace wearing soft garments. Another king will, through his legal representative, succeed where Herod failed and have Jesus put to death as a pretender to the throne. The success of that enterprise would have no more effect than Herod's plotting in stifling the revelation of God in Jesus Christ. All of this took place within the wisdom and counsel of God, as the final dream reminds us. The worst possible interpretation of this event would be an apologetic attempt to understand it within the context of history or science. Those who seek to find the star of Bethlehem in the sky are looking in the wrong place and should be so advised. The bright light of the Epiphany that illuminates the entire world is part of the order of grace rather than nature.

HOMILETICAL INTERPRETATION

First Lesson: Isa. 60:1–6. Israel—a "light to the nations"? How hard that would have been to hear while being held captive in Babylon. But these words "arise, shine" appear to returning exiles on the road back to Jerusalem. How would they be expected to arise or shine? Only because the glory of the Lord had risen—only because their light had come. Into the darkness of Israel's plight shone the glory of the Lord, and the author announces the coming salvation. Theophanies may not mean much in our time, but a manifestation of God's power to postexilic Israel spelled certain salvation. If at other times God appeared as "earthquake, wind, and fire," here he appeared as "light." In preaching on this passage one cannot miss the power of these light-dark images. Unlike our age of fluorescence and floodlights, Isaiah's image approximates the flicker of a candle at the end of a dark cave where not even the backs of our hands are visible. Israel is not only saved by the light; it spreads the light. This humble broken people shall draw all nations unto them. Gentiles and kings shall come together to bask in the warmth and brilliance of the light.

If we stopped here, the sermon could be preached in a synagogue. Giving the OT its due without abruptly placing Christ at the end as a poor rubber stamp is the business of the responsible Christian preacher. Our OT passage anticipates the Christ who floods light into our darkness and manifests the power of God; who gathers all unto him to show that his power and love are universal.

Second Lesson: Eph. 3:1–12. The "mystery of Christ" referred to here is certainly a theological declaration for the early church.

But it is also a political statement—and a revolutionary one. In a time when Jewish Christians and Gentile Christians still found it difficult to "sit at table" with one another, Paul, or more probably, a non-Pauline author, writes that "the Gentiles should be fellow heirs, and of the same body, and partakers of his promise in Christ by the gospel." The statement is theological since Israel the elect is joined by the Gentile nations. If there is not enough mystery in this word alone, the political problem of putting all people together around the same table sharing a common meal under the reign of a common lord further complicates things. People of one church have trouble today breaking bread with people in another, not to speak of those within the same church. This message of the "mystery of Christ," a message of "unity," must be preached, heard, and taken seriously by all in the church. The author of Ephesians sees this as his mission and ours as well. But we achieve this mission only by the grace of God. Again the emphasis is less on what we can do and more on what God has done in Christ Jesus. Only because of Christ can we "sit at table" with one another, can we have unity at all, and preach his word to the Gentiles.

Gospel: Matt. 2:1–12. One cannot avoid being drawn into this story. It has all the elements of a good story: suspense, conflict, human interest, intrigue. And look at the characters: a nervous king and his nervous town, foreign ambassadors, a pretender to the throne in a cradle, a humble Jew and his humble wife who would like to have their baby in peace. Then there's that star, that mysterious star. Astrology is big business these days. People look up in order to look forward. But it was even bigger business in Jesus' time. Here is a quaint story about a star seen in the east by wise men from the East. Why wise men? For Matthew, the truth of Christ's birth comes to Gentiles in Bethlehem, which is the place of the fulfillment of Jewish prophecy. How ironic for non-Jews to find the fulfillment of Jewish prophecy while "all Jerusalem" quakes in fear of this event. The whole story is full of paradox, until one understands that Matthew demonstrates the universal power of the Christ-child as Savior. The star is the common thread that holds the story together. The wise men see it, follow it, and ask about it. Herod scurries about in fear of it and employs his CIA to investigate it. A very curious star—a powerful one, though, for it illumines the world. God has broken in as he has at no other time. This is no "twinkle twinkle" little star. No matter how much we or Herod or the Jews "wish I may, wish I might,"

God shatters all our poor wishes, all our astrological longings with a child who is "born king of the Jews." Why all this stir over the star, then? Maybe the stir was over the child. The baby Jesus made Herod tremble. There is nothing more pitiful than a wealthy or powerful man running scared. God has now come into a humble home, and the very humility of this home and this child are a threat to all the rulers of the world. No matter how much rulers attempt to stamp this child out of our memory, they will, like Herod, fall short. Aside from the prophecy, what unnerved Herod and all Jerusalem is that Gentiles would worship this new king. But the power Jesus had as a child was only a hint of the power he had on the cross. Here the confession of the wise men in v. 2 is heard again on Pilate's lips: "King of the Jews." But what Matthew makes clear is that Jesus is the King of all—Jews and Gentiles.

General Exposition. One is struck by the appeal to unity that appears in the three passages. Gentiles and kings come together in the Isaiah passage. Gentiles shall be fellow heirs in Ephesians. The fellowship is a mystery only given meaning in Christ; Christ is the one who has called us to preach to all the nations. What happens in Matthew to round out the story? The revelation of the Christ-child comes not to Jews but to the magi—Gentiles from the East. But the unity cannot be achieved by man alone. Humankind is marred by sin and unable to come together on its own. Only by God's power and initiative can this great feat be achieved. Only in Jesus Christ do all come together. Then comes the most common denominator— that Jesus is the light that illumines all human experience and shows what God has done and is doing in the world. He is to be worshiped as the magi did, to be followed as the disciples did, to be obeyed as countless have. Without his life none of our lives makes any sense. By his power and authority are we brought together; for the power is greater than the power of kings and his authority greater than presidents'. Here is good news for all to hear and heed. Rejoice in the Lord, for he has done wondrous things!

The Baptism of Our Lord
The First Sunday after the Epiphany

Lutheran	Roman Catholic	Episcopal	Pres/UCC/Chr	Meth/COCU
Isa. 42:1–7	Isa. 42:1–4, 6–7	Isa. 42:1–9	Gen. 1:1–5	Isa. 42:1–9
Acts 10:34–38	Acts 10:34–38	Acts 10:34–38	Eph. 2:11–18	Acts 10:34–38
Luke 3:15–17, 21–22	Luke 3:15–16, 21–22	Luke 3:15–16, 21–22	Luke 3:15–17, 21–22	Luke 3:15–17, 21–22

EXEGESIS

First Lesson: Isa. 42:1–9. Deutero-Isaiah prophesied in the years before the end of the Exile (538 B.C.). The section which begins at 41:1 and ends at 42:9 is a trial of the nations. In it the gods of other countries are found to be nonexistent, despite the power and might displayed by the countries that claimed them as patrons. God alone has charge over human history (41:21–24). Communication of this judgment will be the responsibility of the "servant."

This passage contains the first of the so-called servant songs. These poems were composed separately and later included in the structure of the prophecies. The first closes the trial by introducing the means through which God's judgment will be broadcast. That is why the word *judgment* is repeated three times in these verses (42:1c, 3c, and 4b). Vv. 5–9 are an addition to the song which comments upon its meaning and seeks to make its obscurities clear.

One obscurity not cleared up by either the text or the subsequent verses is the identity of the servant. Interpreters often presume that the prophet had a specific referent in mind which exegesis can discover. Israel itself is perhaps one of the most frequent solutions to this puzzle (see 41:8). Another possibility, however, is that the language of 42:1–4 is intentionally cryptic. The prophet was clear about the means of revelation but unwilling to designate its agent. Such procedures were not uncommon in prophetic and, especially, apocalyptic documents. The "beast" in the Apocalypse (13:1ff.) and the "abomination of desolation" (Mark 13:14) are two examples of deliberate obscurity.

The form of Isa. 42:1–4 refers to a public designation such as kings receive at their coronation rather than the private call which prophets experience. The use of this passage in the Baptism of Jesus bears this out. The servant will function both by actions and by proclamation, combining, so to speak, the roles of judge and prophet. In contrast to political leaders of the normal type, however, he will not achieve his ends by the exercise of sheer power, nor will he have his views published in the manner of royal decrees. The ruler of human events will not operate like those who only presume to control destiny.

Acceptance of God's rule will bring the security and peace that earthly kings cannot. "Blindness" and "imprisonment" are not specifics; they stand for all human suffering, the first symbolizing injuries wrought by nature and the second the wrongs inflicted by people upon one another. Proclamation of this possibility for genuine happiness will be the servant's task. While the conquests wrought by kings lead to acclaim and admiration, the work of the servant will, ironically, bring about his own suffering. The mode of his operation is not good in and of itself, but contrasts the vast difference between divine and human values.

Second Lesson: Acts 10:34–38. These four verses are the opening of Peter's sermon in the home of Cornelius, an address that will be concluded by a miracle in v. 44. Like the Gospel, then, it describes a religious act that will be validated by an immediate intervention of the Spirit. The general context is Luke's elaborate description of the first conversion of a Gentile, 10:1—11:18. The passage as a whole is fairly swamped by Lucan interests and themes. His major thesis is that the Gentile mission did not take its inception from the work of any human being. God goaded the missionaries to make this momentous step. Paul, in particular, had nothing to do with it. The vehicle selected for inaugurating this movement was none other than Peter, leader of the Twelve and first follower of Jesus.

Within this wholly congenial framework 10:36–38 stands out for its preservation of distinctly non-Lucan ideas. They give the exegete a peek behind the scenes of the NT. At the center of these verses is material taken from Second and Third Isaiah and cast into the form of a creed. Acts 10:37–38 is an early Christian confession of faith. It dates the inception of Jesus' messiahship to his Baptism, at which time he was "anointed with Holy Spirit and power" (to work miracles). The Christology here expressed was rejected by later Christians, including Luke, but it does give one clue to the meaning of the Baptism as originally transmitted.

The theme of the sermon as a whole is universalism. Divine impartiality and the worldwide lordship of Christ are set forth by Luke as references to the Gentile mission. In this way the lesson fits the context of the season as well as the specific propers for this Sunday.

Gospel: Luke 3:15–17, 21–22. Luke 3:1–20 contains a summary of the Baptizer's ministry, completing the story begun in chaps. 1 and 2. This account opens with the synchronism, which highlights the transition from introductory to central events (3:1–2), and an expansion of Mark's citation from Isaiah, the purpose of which is to note the universal application of the salvation about to be announced (3:4–6). There follows a summary of the Baptist's teaching and an account of his arrest and detention (3:7–20). By adding vv. 10–14 to the Q account of John's fiery message, Luke toned down John and made him appear more of a teacher of practical, howbeit somewhat radical, ethics. For those who had only this Gospel (and none of the evangelists, it must be remembered, intended their book to be one of four), the thought that John baptized Jesus would be surprising. Luke did not deny this outright but was willing to let his readers think that John was already jailed when Jesus came upon the scene. For early Christians the subordination of Jesus to John was an acute embarrassment (see Matthew and John).

The Baptist's original message was probably not a prediction of a coming Messiah. The "mightier one" was probably God himself. John's actual proclamation threatened imminent judgment by fire (or wind and fire). Christian additions have transformed it into Spirit (in Greek "wind" and "spirit" are the same word) and fire. John used the traditional metaphor of the harvest to describe the coming judgment, comparing the separation of good and evil people to the process by which the wind separated wheat from the chaff that would be burned (vv. 17–18). Luke shifts the fulfillment of this prophecy from the final judgment to the event of Pentecost.

Against any who might be inclined to hail John as the Messiah, Luke added v. 15, thus giving John's message the character of a reply to a question about his own status and a statement about Christology. John denies that he is the one but announces that a Christ is about to come. The meaning of this manipulation of tradition for Christians today is that christological views must be corrected by God's acts rather than continually reiterated in the event of failure. God does not act to cover up for human mistakes, even if they are those of his own prophets. John is regarded as a great saint and hero of the faith. In contemplating this fact we must observe that he does not gain this regard because of the correctness of his views. In fact, everything that he looked for failed to materialize. John is not a saint because he was always right but because he kept faith despite the failure of his private expectations.

As for the actual Baptism, Luke hurries over it as a pious act performed by Jesus, like prayer or temple worship. What was important was the incidental, if you would, descent of the Spirit on this occasion. The third evangelist makes it clear that the event described was not a vision experienced by Jesus but an objective, public event. The idea that baptism brings the gift of the Spirit is Christian. It does not come from John's activity or contemporary Jewish beliefs. The Baptism of Jesus in the Gospels does not describe his adoption as God's Son. It explains why baptism and the Holy Spirit belong together. For this reason there is good warrant for the administration of Holy Baptism on this Sunday.

HOMILETICAL INTERPRETATION

First Lesson: Isa. 42:1–7. There is nothing unique about people being appointed for special jobs today. Israel was no different. Kings, judges, prophets were appointed. What was different about Israel was that God usually had a part in the appointment. In our "secular city" it is often more difficult to talk in these terms. Sometimes even clergy have difficulty talking about the call autobiographically. For Israel this was not a problem. "Behold my servant, whom I uphold" are the words of Yahweh. The language is that of the announcement of a king more than the call of a prophet. And the king appointed here is one of great importance, for God has a part in this appointment: "I have put my Spirit upon him." How odd to employ a royal proclamation to announce an unknown servant! It could be that the author has kept him hidden for a purpose. Whatever the reason, it is difficult not to see Jesus immediately in the passage. The servant brings justice; not the "harsh law of the world" but the justice, the righteousness of God (*mishpat*).

It is interesting to note that this servant does not lift his voice in the street. Lifting one's voice would be kingly action. On the surface one might ask, "Could this be a proof text against modern evangelical techniques, when evangelists argue that Jesus would have gone on television if he had lived today?" The key in this passage is not technique so much as intention. Does one act in humility or is one selling oneself? Certainly this servant is not hiding his light under a bushel. He is to be a beacon to the nations. In this way justice is brought forth in the world. No wonder the power of God is praised. The call of the servant is a sign of God's love for his people.

Second Lesson: Acts 10:34–38. Peter's sermon has a clear message: God plays no favorites. But this passage is first about Christ and then about the way he affects the worldwide mission of the church. The ministry of Christ begins at his Baptism, where he truly becomes a servant appointed by God. As in the servant song, the Holy Spirit comes upon the servant Jesus, who then has the power to "go about doing good." "Going about doing good" sounds ambiguous unless you have read the Gospels and know how this Christ touches the lives of people even today.

All this talk about the power of Christ sounds like so much piety until one reflects on the powerlessness of the state or technology or reason alone to create unity among people—to dispel disharmony. Appeals to our common humanity fall short when blacks and whites are called on to live together in peace, when blue-collar and white-collar workers are asked to give up their greed and make economic amends, when our country and third-world countries are asked to break fiscal bread together. Hence Peter's surprise in v. 28. In the face of the world's powerlessness enters the power of Christ, breaking down barriers and bringing peace to people who have never seen peace. Yes, he "went about doing good." And he still does.

Gospel: Luke 3:15–17, 21–22. The drama in this passage cries out for attention. Will we preachers miss the chance to play with the scene, to dress it up with splashing detail of Jesus' going under for the third time? Luke has no appreciation for our problem. John has presumably been carted off to prison. He is either doing time in the slammer or has already lost his head. Along comes Jesus, seemingly one in a crowd of others being baptized. Maybe Luke is right in playing down the details. Now the emphasis can be put on those opening heavens and the descending dove. The Holy Spirit initiates Jesus' ministry and mission—not John. The Holy Spirit gives him God's special brand of power—echoes of Isaiah, "I have put my Spirit upon him." As in the servant song, Christ is the chosen one ("Thou art my beloved Son") designated by the power of God to carry out God's work in the world.

As Christ gains significance, John fades from the picture. John

clearly subordinates himself to Jesus. John has played his role and
exits from the stage to make room for the main figure of the Lucan
drama, the central character of the dramatic history of salvation.

General Exposition. If Epiphany spells the unfolding manifestation of Christ, this Sunday's sermon must keep its focus on Christ.
Today is not a day to preach about the nature of the church or how
we can be better Christians, although those are related themes. Today
we are called to preach "not ourselves but Christ," his Baptism, his
mission, his ministry. John understood that.

Who is this Christ we preach? He is Lord of *all*—a recurrent theme
in this season and crucial to Luke's Gospel. Of course, a worldwide
mission sounds nice until taken seriously. This Christ challenges
homogeneity, whether it be in suburban community or establishment
church. To talk of a Christ who disregards rank or social status is
rather dangerous. Imagine singing,

> In Christ there is no East or West,
> No this side of the tracks or that,
> No welfare line, no country club,
> No crown, and no hard hat.

To many this is nonsense, because the world yawns at the power
of the Holy Spirit which came upon Christ; yet this power can effect
change and bring peace among peoples. Because of the Spirit, Christ
rules not as a king but as a servant, not lording it over us but calling
us to be humble servants as well. Yes, Christ "went about doing
good," because "God was with him." God is with us too.

The Second Sunday after the Epiphany

Lutheran	Roman Catholic	Episcopal	Pres/UCC/Chr	Meth/COCU
Isa. 62:1–5	Isa. 62:1–5	Isa. 62:1–5	Isa. 62:2–5	Isa. 62:1–5
1 Cor. 12:1–11	1 Cor. 12:4–11	1 Cor. 12:1–11	1 Cor. 12:4–11	1 Cor. 12:1–11
John 2:1–11	John 2:1–12	John 2:1–11	John 2:1–12	John 2:1–12

EXEGESIS

First Lesson: Isa. 62:1–5. Chap. 62 is a single poem, of which this lesson contains the first two strophes (vv. 1–3 and 4–5). The larger unit of which this is a piece runs from chap. 60 through 62. Its form is that of a community lament. Note also the chiastic (A B B A) structure of vv. 4–5.

Jerusalem's present condition will be reversed. Change of name is symbolic of a new relationship and altered status. At least two of the names used, Azubah, "forsaken," and Beulah, "married," were actual proper names for women. Marriage was a conventional image for the relationship between God and Israel, and was taken up also by the church.

In this lesson the thought is that of remarriage, not the restoration of a broken relationship. This implies discontinuity and newness more than a return to the previous state of affairs. Because the entire community plays the role of "bride," individualization of the concept to describe the relationship between God and a believer is bad exegesis. Furthermore, the notion is not that of a union between equal partners, as in present-day marriage, but of the bride as quite dependent and utterly submissive.

For Christians the analogy is the covenant between God and the church, a covenant which believers enter at Baptism. One's relation to God is not simply personal. It occurs within a community structure and in a communal setting. In line with the season the lesson uses the motifs of light and of God's appearance.

Second Lesson: 1 Cor. 12:1–11. First Corinthians will be used for the New Testament Lesson during all of the "ordinary" Sundays after Epiphany. The portions selected deal with the nature of Christian life in this world. The overriding issue may be liturgically expressed as an examination of the way in which believers manifest the divine in daily life. Many of the Corinthians were deeply attracted to the possibilities inherent in what we would call "Pentecostal" experiences. Unlike most modern Pentecostals, however, these Corinthian "pneumatics" were intellectually oriented and inclined toward a very "progressive" life-style. Socially they were upwardly mobile and apt to be snobbish.

The specific subject of most of these lessons deals with spiritual gifts, what they are, how they are to be evaluated, and to what degree they demonstrate one's possession of heavenly reality. Paul is carrying on a discussion with his own converts. His authority is not in question. When confronted by excess, the apostle does not prohibit. He tends, instead, to place such activities in their proper perspective. Paul's thesis comes in 12:1-3. Vv. 4-31 go on to discuss the multiplicity and unity of spiritual gifts.

Because ecstasy and the like are not confined to Christianity but are, as we would say, "phenomena in the history of religions," they do not prove that one has the Spirit. Only the ability to recite the Creed can do that. Confession of Jesus as Lord is not an individual choice or the affirmation of a theological system. It is a miracle (vv. 1-3). All other gifts are subordinate to this, which constitutes the decisive criterion.

Vv. 4-6 are a triadic unit. "The Spirit" is correlated with "spiritual gifts" (Gr. *charismata*), "the Lord" with "acts of service," and "God" to "(miraculous) operations." Paul thus places humble acts of everyday service on the same level as extraordinary marvels. The reason for this is that divine standards differ from human. The Spirit creates the community (Body) and distributes gifts according to the common needs (v. 7). What counts, then, is value for the community, not individual triumphs. A list of possible gifts follows, including those related to teaching and theologizing, miracles of various sorts, and ecstatic prophecy. Last in this catalog is the gift of tongues and its interpretation. This is surprising, not least to the Corinthians, who would have placed it at the top. Paul's order was not accidental. He valued this item least because it was the least edifying of the items mentioned, being unintelligible and prone to convince its practitioners that they were enjoying the angelic life (cf. 13:1). V. 12:11 reminds the hearers that all gifts are due to the will of the Spirit and have nothing to do with human ability or merit. They can be no source for pride. The repeated adjective "one" in connection with the Spirit underlines the fact that the Spirit works within the Body to maintain unity in diversity.

Gospel: John 2:1–12. Gods show their nature by the manner in which they reveal themselves. Wine miracles were thus favorite means of revelation for wine-gods like Dionysus, who by this gift brought people relaxation and release from the tedium of daily existence. In the period when Christianity came into being, gods often took over the virtues and attributes of their competitors as a means for claiming to be the universal, chief deity. John 2:1ff. implicitly proclaims the replacement or supersession of pagan and Jewish religion in the wine miracle and explicitly so in the reference to purification (v. 6) and the contrast between old and new in v. 10.

The point of this story as it is found in John lies not in the miracle. The account has been edited to give it a new twist. One change appears to have been the addition of the disciples (vv. 2 and 11). Originally this story was of a "domestic" sort, like Luke 2:41–52. V. 3 is another addition. In the immediate context it means that miracle workers cannot be manipulated. For the Gospel as a whole the "hour" of Jesus is his Passion. The insertion of this phrase relativizes the subsequent wonder by reminding us that all Jesus did in the way of miracles did not prevent his Crucifixion. God has more in store for us than the alleviation of household shortages.

The end of the account is quite unusual. One expects the fact of the miracle to become public and all to react in approval. On the contrary, the source of this wine remains a secret to all but the servants. Miracle workers may refuse to be manipulated, but there is little point to a miracle that remains unknown. (V. 9b is another addition. It raises the question of Jesus' origin. See also 7:27–28; 8:14; 9:29–30; and 19:9.)

The point of the episode is that the best comes last. All the guests know is that the better wine did come later. In this sense the miracle does reveal Jesus' nature as the bringer of new revelation. V. 11 is a typical conclusion to a miracle, but those who are said to have come to faith are not the witnesses to the miracle, so that the miracle is not used in the typical way. Therefore it is not correct to state that Jesus revealed his glory and provoked faith by turning water into wine. The account is much more subtle. When the wine appears, its character as revelation is visible only to the eyes of faith.

It is unlikely that John 2:1–12 had a sacramental intent, although application of the new revelation to the Eucharist is certainly legitimate. The theme of marriage provides an obvious link to the First Lesson. If the parish or congregation has the custom of solemnizing Holy Matrimony at the Sunday liturgy, this occasion would be highly appropriate for such a celebration.

HOMILETICAL INTERPRETATION

First Lesson: Isa. 62:1–5. The wedding bells are ringing in today's passages. In Isaiah, salvation is imminent. Israel is about to return to her own land and to her Lord. There is reason for rejoicing. Like all metaphors about God and his people, this one cannot and should not be pushed. Theological language is ordinary language used in extraordinary ways. It is the language of human experience expanded to help man understand God more clearly. But it often falls short. Here the marriage image gives us a glimpse of God and his relationship to Israel.

In this passage our light-dark images emerge again as well. Israel's "vindication goes forth as brightness, and her salvation as a burning torch." Why should a beaten, frustrated, confused people trudging home from Babylon burn so brightly? Because of their sure knowledge that salvation was imminent. How has Israel been saved? By the grace of God. Emphasis in preaching this passage must be placed here. There would be no return, no glory, no brightness, no burning torch, no "crown of beauty," no "royal disdain" but for the unmerited grace of God. He is the source of salvation and the giver of it as well.

Second Lesson: 1 Cor. 12:1–11. The Pauline metaphor here is appropriate in the season of Epiphany. Its talk of the same spirit continues the stress on unity with the Holy Spirit as the source of that unity. One is reminded of the problem Paul addresses in 1 Cor. 1:10–17 where the groups follow certain leaders. One could almost supply the name of one's favorite TV evangelist or hometown preacher and make the story more contemporary. In the same way, when one believes oneself to be superior to another because of spiritual gifts, then dissension arises. Christ's Body becomes a giant jigsaw puzzle where none of the pieces ever quite fits. "Is Christ divided?" Our ministry is diverse but it should never be divisive— different gifts but the same Spirit. Today we hear echoes of this problem: "I'm a fundamentalist; I'm a social activist; I speak in tongues, don't you?" Paul is not against glossolalia or scholarly exegesis. But when one is lorded over another, the Body of Christ suffers internal hemorrhaging. Paul does not attack spiritual gifts but unjustified spiritual pride. Gifts are only the manifestation of the Spirit. The Spirit is what counts.

Gospel: John 2:1–12. John's Gospel is probably the most difficult to preach, because of the layers of floating logia. The wedding at Cana pericope is no exception. Because of the layers of meaning and levels of symbolism, it is almost easier to talk about what this passage is *not* homiletically than what it is. It is not a miracle story in the classic sense of that in the Synoptics. It is not a story of Jesus' insensitivity or on the general topic of "how not to treat your mother." Furthermore, it is not more insight into Jesus as a man: "How Jesus Acts at Parties." But at the same time the passage points to the person of Jesus which is manifested in his actions. This first of John's signs is told to reveal Jesus in his glory. Why? So that his disciples will believe. Everything in the passage leads to v. 11: the empty jars, the miracle, the choice new wine, his statement that hints at the cross, his placing his ministry before natural family relationships. Jesus replaces the old order. His disciples understand him and see him in his glory.

General Exposition. The preacher is faced with many problems if he wants to bring all three passages together. The Johannine passage seeks to demonstrate Christ in his glory to bring the disciples to assent and faith. It would be difficult enough to preach by itself without putting it together with the other two. The Pauline passage is more pneumatological. But it also stresses the unity of the church in the same Spirit. Certainly the Holy Spirit is upon Christ, empowering him to speak and act with authority in the name of the Father. But the Johannine passage does not mention the Spirit. In addition, John has a different agenda and a different intention. At the same time, however, when two authors are emphasizing specific ideas for specific audiences, it is our responsibility as preachers to determine whether or not one will be more appropriate on a given Sunday or with a given church than another.

I would find it difficult to preach on the Isaiah passage without at some point moving to the NT. Zion may have had its glory, but now God is manifesting his glory in Jesus, who will replace the rituals and functions of Israel. I would not make too much of the wedding imagery for fear that the central motif of both passages (Isaiah and

John) would get lost in the partying. The three passages offer good themes for Epiphany, but placing all of them together could create either a confusing collage or a very long sermon.

The Third Sunday after the Epiphany

Lutheran	Roman Catholic	Episcopal	Pres/UCC/Chr	Meth/COCU
Isa. 61:1–6	Neh. 8:2–4a, 5–6, 8–10	Neh. 8:2–10	Neh. 8:1–3, 5–6, 8–10	Neh. 8:1–4a, 5–6, 8–10
1 Cor. 12:12–21, 26–27	1 Cor. 12:12–30 or 1 Cor. 12:12–14, 27	1 Cor. 12:12–27	1 Cor. 12:12–30	1 Cor. 12:12–30
Luke 4:14–21	Luke 1:1–4; 4:14–21	Luke 4:14–21	Luke 4:14–21	Luke 1:1–4; 4:14–21

EXEGESIS

First Lesson: Neh. 8:2–10. This passage, which properly includes Neh. 7:73b—8:12 (as paragraphed in RSV), is probably out of place in Ezra-Nehemiah. It is a continuation of the Ezra story. The later addition of Nehemiah and the Levites to v. 9 brought representatives of state and temple into the account.

The scene described is one of great solemnity, although not a religious service proper. Ezra, flanked by six notables on either side, proclaims the Torah to a large assembly. Just what was read is not certain. It could not have been the entire Pentateuch. The time allotted would not even allow for one of the principal strands (viz., the D account). The role of the Levites would have included both translation (from Hebrew into Aramaic, the lingua franca of the Persian Empire) and exposition. The ceremonies resemble those used by many Christians for the solemn proclamation of the Gospel.

The reading of Torah was in fact "gospel," and not just "law." Ezra exhorted the people that repentance for their shortcomings was not to be their only response. Joy at God's revealed care for humanity and repeated acts of mercy is likewise necessary. The proper response for the proclamation of God's message is celebration, even if the message does not sound like a cause for immediate happiness.

Second Lesson: 1 Cor. 12:12–30. For the general context see under the Second Sunday after the Epiphany. The issue here is differentiation and the tendency to settle the difficulties caused by differentiation through the assignment of rank. Paul combats the desire of many Corinthians to use religious spectacularity as the basis for ranking. He resists this attempt to elevate certain individuals by invoking a traditional political metaphor in which the citizen body is compared to a living organism. Vv. 12–27 are marked as a unit by the device of *inclusio*, similar opening and closing phrases.

Paul inverts the metaphor as it normally appears. The conventional argument was that the body politic gained its form from the association of various components. Ancient writers used this image to justify social hierarchy by asserting, as it were, that even a sophisticated machine requires cogs, which may then suffer in silent satisfaction. They are lowly but necessary. Paul begins by asserting that the body is a priori and differentiation is secondary (v. 12). The body is not just a social organization; it is a supernatural entity into which people are incorporated by baptism, which allows no distinctions (v. 13). Eschatologically, there are absolutely no differences, and that is all that counts. Empirically, however, differences presently exist (vv. 14–15). To this issue Paul will now speak.

The thrust of his message comes in vv. 15–16, where it is important to note that the phrase "out of the body" refers both to the proud claims of individuals to have transcended the limits of bodily existence through spiritual performances and to individualism. That is, "body" here means both the body of a person and the Body of Christ. Paul contends that all Christians are charismatic by virtue of the gift of the Spirit (baptism) which brings to all the possibility of life together (Eucharist). All functions thus have equal validity from both the corporate and the charismatic perspectives. Paul does *not* criticize Corinthians for being "Pentecostal." What he attacks is the tendency to elitism and individualism that some have pursued. Ecstasy which leads away from the Body of Christ is not "spiritual," for the real miracle is incorporation, not disembodiment. He has thus laid the groundwork for chap. 13, which will go on to explain and praise this greatest of all spiritual miracles.

Ranking thus applies only to "apostles, prophets and teachers," who have particular calls. The rest of the functions are equally necessary for the health of the Body (vv. 28–30). From this it becomes clear that a willingness to wash the dishes may be a far more Christian charisma than the ability to give a virtuoso performance that leaves others uncertain of their status and faith.

Gospel: Luke 4:14–21. Luke 4:14—9:50 contains the Galilean ministry of Jesus. This passage is its grand opening, an episode that is divided into two weeks' readings. Vv. 4:14–15 derive from Mark 1:14–15. Comparison reveals Luke's concern to play down Mark's view of the imminence of the kingdom. In 4:16–30 the inaugural scene proper takes place.

Since the source for this narrative was Mark 6:1–6a, it is apparent that the narrative is basically Luke's own composition. The method followed here was characteristic of what he did in Acts, but unusual for the Gospel. It is a full-length story, including a sermon, crowd reaction, an adventure, and a close escape. Breaking the account up into two readings is thus inconvenient, to say the least.

Luke followed this unusual procedure because he wished to high-light the inception of Jesus' public ministry in a dramatically effective way. The scene is typical and ideal, for it is more concerned to fore-shadow Jesus' life and fate and the later experience of the church's mission than to give a factual report handed down by early followers. That is why the closest parallel to this story comes from the mission-ary journey reported in Acts 13—14.

Proper synagogue procedure is not at issue. Jesus assumes the right to read and, apparently, selects his own "text." The quotation would not have come from any normal Bible, for it is a combination of Isa. 62:1–2, with an omission, and Isa. 58:6, with a modification. From this one may gather that the quotation is a Christian text, the purpose of which was to serve as a summary of the gospel. In its present set-ting v. 18 refers to the Baptism (cf. Acts 10:38), at which time Jesus was filled with the power to preach and work miracles (4:14). The readers know the meaning of this passage, and the eager expectation described in v. 20 stems from their understanding. V. 21 is, as the following indicates, intended to be a summary of Jesus' message, which was an announcement that he was the Messiah of whom Isaiah (presumably) spoke. For what will happen next one must come back again the following Sunday.

HOMILETICAL INTERPRETATION

First Lesson: Neh. 8:2–10. Examples of hurried exegesis and "word-association" preaching filled the pulpits of this country a few years ago when this text was read and preached. The stories of Ezra's Water Gate and Nixon's Watergate may be symptomatic of the sin rampant in both lands, but aside from the name, that is the only con-nection. This passage is about the law—the reading, the hearing, and the obeying of it. The law is for all: "men and women and all who could hear with understanding." The scene cries out for attention. There is a drama to it as Ezra opens the Torah: all eyes are on him and "all the ears of the people were attentive to the book of the law." What preacher would not be jealous?

One could easily concentrate on the people in this story: Ezra reading the law, the Levites helping to interpret it, the people weeping as they comprehend its meaning, and finally the feasting and partying when Ezra makes clear the function of the law. For the Jew it is indeed good news. Civil law may not be good news, but God's law can be and is. This is one reason James Sanders talks of Torah as gospel. Surely the day is holy when news such as this is delivered. What else is there to do but celebrate? Of course, we stand on this side of the cross. Jesus Christ fulfills that law and goes beyond it—even more reason for Christians to rejoice. Calvin's third use of the law is a call to obedience in response to the salvation offered in Jesus Christ. Here the believer is called to lead a joyous, holy life as a result of God's mercy.

Finally, one cannot talk about the law without talking about God who is the giver of the law. No matter how much we want to preach the people and their reactions to Ezra's preaching, a sermon on this passage cannot avoid bringing people to an awareness of God's presence and action in the law.

Second Lesson: 1 Cor. 12:12–30. Many members, one Body. That sounds simple enough. But there is always a catch. Paul never makes things that simple. What are we to do with all this body language? Paul seems to move from body language to Body theology without missing a beat. It ought to be appealing today, with jogging tracks and health spas brimming with anxious people, not to mention nonverbal communication courses at the local community college or university. But Paul has something else in mind. He is not interested in how people cross their arms to resist or stare at the numbers on an elevator. He is trying to describe the church. Like every analogy between human experience and divine reality, this one must not be pushed too far. Paul is only providing a context for his argument. What is crucial is that one person or group should not perceive itself as superior to others, for in God's plan all are alike. No one can think that the whole church's existence hinges on him or her. Ecclesiastical leaders—clergy and laity—sometimes feel this way. Leander Keck calls this group the "church bureaucrats." They have been in this business so long they can't imagine doing anything else. The church will rise or fall on their actions. Anyone who falls into this trap thinks too highly of self and dismisses the power of the Holy Spirit. Paul is also especially keen to bring back into line people whose spiritual escapades have pushed them into a kind of Gnostic dualism. They see themselves as superior to others because of their knowledge gained by "spiritual" experience. Gnostic perfectionism often leads to elitism. This stress on unity continues one of the important themes of the Epiphany season.

Gospel: Luke 4:14–21. It is difficult to treat this passage without adding vv. 22–30. Here we get the full picture of the response to Jesus' sermon. The lectionary choices create a serial effect as with a two-part story. "Tune in next week," we are told. What we have before us then is a return home to Nazareth, the reading of a text and a sermon, very brief. What follows next week is totally unexpected.

Aside from the powerful drama of the scene, three things are crucial here. First, Jesus' ministry is empowered by the Spirit—something we have heard before in this Epiphany season. Without the Spirit, Jesus' ministry is empty and powerless. Second, Jesus *fulfills* the salvation talked of in the Isaiah passage. Not only that, he fulfills and replaces Jewish law. We do not see this the way the Jews did, for so many of us are lurking Marcionites masquerading as Christians. When will we learn that our story did not begin with the Crucifixion or at Pentecost, but with a tired Jew named Abraham trudging about a Middle Eastern desert? Third, there is a social dimension here that is too often overlooked. Preaching good news to the poor and proclaiming release to the captives is not exactly safe, conservative practice. This passage taken seriously creates tension for middle-class America. Certainly the salvation is spiritual, but is it not much more? The answers are not easy. They are more complex than liberation theology would make them, although its critique must be taken seriously.

General Exposition. Preaching could include all three passages, but the Lucan text should stand as the centerpiece. Jesus is the center of our ministry. With the OT and the law on the one side and the church and its mission on the other, Jesus is the center of our attention. Preaching these passages could deal with a contrast, with ministry and the Spirit, or with the Pauline metaphor of the body.

The contrast is between the story of Ezra and the account of Jesus in the synagogue. They seem similar. Ezra reads and expounds the law. Jesus reads and interprets the Isaiah passage. In both, the audience is concerned with the meaning of tradition to which they give assent. However, in the first story the audience weeps and then weeping turns to joy, whereas in the story of Jesus, praise turns to rage. In Ezra's story, all understand the meaning. After Jesus' sermon, all misunderstand his mission. Maybe the problem is that they understand too well!

But preaching on this contrast alone would take the congregation away from the central theme—who Jesus Christ is and what his purpose is on earth. His purpose is spelled out in the Isaiah passage. Jesus has not come to hobnob with the rich; he has come to bring salvation to the poor. When Jesus stated that the passage was fulfilled in their hearing, he meant it. To proclaim this kind of salvation was to bring it into existence. Without the Spirit this act would not have been efficacious. Without the Spirit our ministry would not be so, either. One cannot read this passage without facing the fact that Jesus' announcement of his ministry calls us as well. But we cannot carry it on as long as the church is separated; as long as the Body of Christ remains disembodied. If one lords oneself over another, the church's mission to the world is hindered. If we do not recognize the pain of other members within our Body, then all of us suffer.

The Fourth Sunday after the Epiphany

Lutheran	Roman Catholic	Episcopal	Pres/UCC/Chr	Meth/COCU
Jer. 1:4–10	Jer. 1:4–5, 17–19	Jer. 1:4–10	Jer. 1:4–10	Jer. 1:4–10, 17–19
1 Cor. 12:27—13:13	1 Cor. 12:31—13:13 or 1 Cor. 13:4–13	1 Cor. 14:12b–20	1 Cor. 13:1–13	1 Cor. 12:27—13:13
Luke 4:21–32	Luke 4:21–30	Luke 4:21–32	Luke 4:22–30	Luke 4:21–32

EXEGESIS

First Lesson: Jer. 1:4–10. Jeremiah was called by God in the thirteenth year of Josiah, probably 627 B.C. He remained active for nearly fifty years. This is the story of how he became a prophet. There is a correct form for the story of the call of a prophet. The experience is a private one, normally in a time of ecstatic trance. Of all the pro-

phetic calls related in the OT (see also Isa. 6 and Ezra 1—3), this had
the strongest influence on the NT, for Paul cited it to describe his
own calling (Gal. 1:15–16) and Luke relied upon this passage for his
own understanding of the missionary vocation (see Acts 9, 22,
and 26).

As is customary, the call takes the form of a dialogue between God
and the prophet. In addition to the voice, there was apparently a
visionary element (v. 9). One purpose of the form is to make it clear
that the call came from God alone without human initiative (v. 5).
Thus it is conventional for the one called to express his or her
unworthiness for the assignment. God does not depend upon such
factors, which in any case are based upon assessments that have no
relation to divine requirements. The extremely realistic language of
v. 9 is the climax: prophets did not merely speak God's will in their
terms; they were the mouthpiece for oracles dropped from heaven.

Jeremiah's message, it is stated at the very beginning, will include
salvation as well as judgment, reward no less than punishment (v. 10).
The parallel with the opening scene in Nazareth is obvious. In the
context of the post-Epiphany season, Jeremiah's role as a prophet to
the nations (vv. 4 and 10) should not be overlooked. God does not
work for the benefit of one group alone.

EPISCOPAL
I Cor. 14:12b-20
see page 36

Second Lesson: 1 Cor. 12:27—13:13. For the opening section
consult the previous section on the Third Sunday after the Epiphany.
Paul lists a number of gifts that many would value highly indeed, and
then urges his readers to seek gifts still more valuable. His description of those gifts was something of a literary tour de force, as no one
needs to be told. What is easy to escape notice is that his suggestion
is a bombshell.

Thematically, chap. 13 is an interruption. In content 14 follows
smoothly after 12. Paul elected this point to interrupt his narrative
with a most arresting digression. Stylistically, the passage is rhetorical,
flashy, and sometimes elegant. It makes use of such devices as asso-
nance, anaphora, and chiasmus. Formally, it resembles prose "hymns"
celebrating the most important deity or virtue. The immediate background was the Hellenized Jewish wisdom tradition. See the hymns in
Proverbs 8, Sirach 24, Wisdom of Solomon 7, and 1 Esd. 4:34–40.
Many of the Corinthian Christians found the wisdom movement quite
intellectually stimulating, as the first four chapters of the letter bear
out. Chap. 13 is thus an example of the type of material they admired.
By this display of virtuosity Paul could capture his audience. They
are left defenseless for the "knockout punch" that chap. 14 will bring.

Vv. 1–7 pursue the standard line of such hymns by claiming that the highest virtue (here "love") is the medium through which all other virtues come to fruition. In the following verses the tone becomes polemical. Love is superior to other virtues. The basis for value is eschatology, the heavenly, as all would agree. Paul states that tongues and the like are good but that they do not belong to the permanent, eternal order. Many in Corinth had thought otherwise, believing that in ecstatic states they had a temporary taste of heaven. Paul said that such moments were only temporal, in both senses of that word. He drove this inversion of values home by playing on the child-adult and shadow-reality themes so beloved of mystics and sages (vv. 11–12). Speaking in tongues is not advanced; it is puerile, a dull reflection of heavenly truth.

The thesis of this chapter, then, is that love is the only eschatological gift presently shared by believers in the full degree. The implications of this statement go far beyond the resolution of a pastoral issue or two. The addition of faith and hope in the last verse stand as a warning that interpreters could scarcely do worse than to reduce this idea of Christian love to mere moralizing or sentimentality.

Gospel: Luke 4:21–32. These verses complete the episode in Nazareth begun in the Gospel for the previous Sunday. On the passage in general please consult that section above. In order to epitomize at the very outset the fate of Jesus, Luke wished to combine the themes of triumph and rejection. Achievement of this end led him into the inconsistency of vv. 22–23, where great admiration gives place to quite unmotivated rejection and brings Jesus to threaten his hearers. There are several other literary problems, all of which underline the ideal character of the scene and the importance for Luke of making his point regardless of the difficulties it raised.

The proverbs cited in vv. 23–24 are the means for providing a transition. Instead of speaking to the issue of Nazareth versus Capernaum or about people rejecting their local prophets, Jesus counters doubts by mentioning two examples from the Elijah-Elisha cycle. In each of these two cases the persons favored were Gentiles (1 Kings 17 and 2 Kings 5). By threatening that rejection by his own people the Jews (here symbolized by Jesus' fellow townsmen) will lead to benefits for Gentiles, Jesus was not referring to events that Luke will later relate regarding his own ministry. He was speaking of the Gentile mission that, according to Acts, the church will begin once Jews have rebuffed God's offer.

The very thought of letting Gentiles in reduces the synagogue crowd

to a frenzy, and they seek to lynch Jesus (cf. Acts 7:57–58 and
14:19), but he eludes their efforts and makes a miraculous escape
(cf. John 8:59; 10:17–18). The reference to an execution "outside the
city" in v. 29 calls the Crucifixion to mind. Thus Luke foreshadows
both the Lord's Passion and the mission of the church. Historically
the account is a Lucan invention. Theologically, it testifies to the fact
that the career of Jesus was not a series of triumphs with an execution
at the end. By his ministry he provoked the authorities to act. Furthermore, this Gospel reminds the church that her fate and that of her
Lord are, in the last analysis, to be one and the same.

HOMILETICAL INTERPRETATION

First Lesson: Jer. 1:4–10. This passage sounds remarkably like
a young candidate for the ministry stammering in the pulpit and bab-
bling objections about being there in the first place. Here is Jeremiah,
tongue-tied, trying to duck behind the "I'm too young, Lord" excuse.
His reticence is met with an announcement of divine initiative and
an authentication of his right to speak for the Lord, his right to
preface his sermons with "Thus saith the Lord." Not only that, the
Lord promises him divine assistance in his homiletical preparation—
the words will be given at the appropriate time. This dialogue between
God and the prophet is intriguing and appealing. Jeremiah has been
chosen long ago, picked out for a special task. If a sermon on this
passage dealt heavily with Jeremiah's feelings of being done in with
no escape, it would miss the point. The point here is not Jeremiah's
problem but God's initiative. God is the one who calls prophets, who
set Jesus on his way ministering to the world, who calls us to work
in his name. No matter how appealing Jeremiah's call is as a personal
story of anguish and occupational crisis, the passage itself concentrates
on God and his power to call and move people into his work in the
world. "Before I formed you in the womb I knew you, and before
you were born I consecrated you." Nevertheless the words of the Lord
still come as comfort: "Be not afraid of them, for I am with you to
deliver you, says the Lord." We need these words, for the ones we
preach are uncomfortable—words of judgment. If the church dodges
this message, the word of the Lord is neither heard nor spoken. But
the word of judgment is always finally a word of salvation. Many
"prophetic" preachers tend to forget that. What is the last line of
v. 10? ". . . to build and to plant." Without this line, judgment is
preached only as harsh law and never as mercy that grows from a
pastor's heart and has its source in the grace of God.

Second Lesson: 1 Cor. 12:27—13:13. This passage is one of the most beloved, most quoted, and best known of any in the Bible. It takes us back to Sunday-school days when we sat all wiggles in that little chair listening to that kindly teacher tell us about faith, hope, and love, but "the greatest of these is love." We remember talk of eros, philia, and agape. Eros and philia were fine, but agape was what counted. But agape sounded so harmless and powerless, so idealistic. Nothing could be further from the truth. Agape is not some soft-hearted love, but one that is tough-minded and realistic about the kind of world we live in. "Love one another" is not bleeding-heart liberalism but a hard word for people who don't want to speak to those around them—much less love them. So an agape feast, as it was celebrated in the early church, is a radical idea. It means sharing food and drink with those you would normally shun. This love is a gift; we would not come upon it on our own. But Paul argues that it is the greatest gift—to be held above all others. Whatever gift a church member has that preempts his capacity to love is for naught, accord-ing to Paul. Not even vows of poverty measure up to this love. No amount of knowledge will do. The phrase "but have not love" echoes as a quiet, haunting refrain, followed by the starkness of these words: "I am nothing." If this was not convincing to those who missed the mark in Paul's Corinthian church, nothing would be. Aside from the hypnotic effect of the poetic rhythms here, the remarkable thing about this passage is its message that love lasts. In a world where change is constant, where economic and political stability are only transitory, this is a remarkable word. Nations have come and gone; kings and rulers have come and gone; we shall soon be gone; but this love lasts. To understand the incredible lasting power of this love in Christ Jesus is to come to a new maturity in our Christian faith.

Gospel: Luke 4:21–32. Going home is never really the same, especially if you have made it big in the public arena. In this case the hometown boy is greeted with rejection and resistance. Jesus came home to Nazareth to announce the beginning of his campaign. He presents his platform: "to preach good news to the poor . . . to pro-claim release to the captives . . . recovering of sight to the blind, to set at liberty those who are oppressed, to proclaim the acceptable year of the Lord." No wonder he didn't get many votes. To those in power his was a radical message. At first the response was favorable (v. 22), but as he spelled out his platform, the crowd became restless and the cheers turned to jeers and a lynch mob arose (hints of a lynching to come). This passage was not only platform speech but inauguration

—the inauguration of the ministry of the Son of God. How odd, but how typical that it should be shrouded in criticism and controversy. Christ is proclaiming the commencement of the time of salvation. As with last week's passage, the same themes of Spirit, Jesus' fulfillment, and the social dimension still obtain. If the Spirit had not been upon him, then his campaign would have failed and his words would have been "mere political rhetoric." But the Spirit was upon him from the beginning. Luke makes clear that Jesus is the Spirit-filled Messiah.

It is unimportant how Walter Cronkite or John Chancellor would have reported this announcement of a public campaign. Luke gives us his report as one of the three major New Testament networks. His bias is clear but not inconsistent with the whole biblical witness when talking of Christ. Jesus is the one who is concerned for all and expects us as his church to be so as well. The words are uncomfortable ones; and somehow they will not go away. Nevertheless they lie defiantly on the page—a written testimony of our Lord's message to us. Just as Jesus' words in another place, "Love your enemies," cause us to squirm, so the announcement of his ministry calls our very way of living into question.

General Exposition. Consider the similarities between Jesus' public announcement and Jeremiah's call. Both are aware that they have been predestined to speak and act for God. Both have a message of judgment and salvation. Both have missions that expand God's work beyond the bounds of the Jewish community. Jeremiah is a prophet to the nations, and Luke's Jesus embarks on a worldwide mission. He moves among the Gentiles even though he is a Jew himself. With Jewish rejection of Jesus, Luke is able to make this point clearly. The focus on preaching to it should not be Jewish rejection, lest we fall into anti-Semitism, but on the universal character of Jesus' mission. Both Jeremiah and Jesus become the mouthpiece of God, but Jesus in an even more real way: "Today this Scripture has been fulfilled in your hearing."

If there are similarities between Jeremiah's call and Jesus' announcement, there is contrast in our analogy of a political campaign. A successful candidate ends his campaign amidst a roaring crowd, a festive celebration. Christ ends his campaign on a cross. But even here there is a victory—victory in defeat. The party comes later with the disciples, and even later at Pentecost. So the campaign doesn't end on a cross but is carried on by the church. Christ's name appears on political banners throughout the world, and the symbol of his love stands defiantly atop our steeples. It is that love to which Paul attests in his famous chapter thirteen. Christ now calls us to make his love real in the world. There is no sentimentality here—"What the world needs now is love, sweet love." Christ lived and died in our world. But he rose above it with a message that met the world where it lived—in its pain and in its joy. We are called with his help to do nothing less. This may be what Jesus had in mind when he presented his platform in that little Nazareth synagogue.

The Fifth Sunday after the Epiphany

Lutheran	Roman Catholic	Episcopal	Pres/UCC/Chr	Meth/COCU
Isa. 6:1–8 (9–13)	Isa. 6:1–8	Judg. 6:11–24a	Isa. 6:1–8	Isa. 6:1–13
1 Cor. 14:12b–20	1 Cor. 15:1–11 or 1 Cor. 15:3–8, 11	1 Cor. 15:1–11	1 Cor. 15:1–11	1 Cor. 15:1–11 or 1 Cor. 14:12b–20
Luke 5:1–11	Luke 5:1–11	Luke 5:1–11	Luke 5:1–11	Luke 5:1–11

EXEGESIS

First Lesson: Isa. 6:1–13. The text dates Isaiah's call precisely to the last year of King Uzziah, around 740 B.C. In the passage assigned, vv. 12–13 are a secondary addition, and the hopeful conclusion to v. 13 is still later yet. The call, which should be compared to Jeremiah's, may be outlined as follows: vision (1–4), preparation (5–7), and call-commission (8–11).

The vision took place in the context of worship. The throne is that on which the ark rested, and the altar of incense provides smoke and a coal for the purification. Isaiah's call was both a personal and a liturgical experience. Dichotomies between cult and true obedience are convenient homiletic devices, but they often overlook the nature of the religious life. In this vision are some of the traditional elements of an epiphany: earthquake, light, and smoke. The seraphim are fabulous figures who nonetheless shield their eyes and genitals (covering one's feet) in God's presence. They too are in awe of the divine. Their hymn is the celebration of God's wondrous presence, as the church has long recognized. The Sanctus is quite properly sung, following reference to the angelic orders, at the beginning of the Eucharistic Prayer. "Hosts" has created a problem for modern translators. Originally it referred to the assembly of heavenly creatures who have been reduced to the role of God's servants.

Whereas Jeremiah had been consecrated prior to his birth (1:5), Isaiah was purified after his vision. Despite what he said, the text describes a vision of only the hem of God's garment. The anthropomorphism is not important. God is so awesome that the glimpse of the merest part of his accoutrements was enough to overcome the believer with fear and reverence. Because of his purification following the vision, Isaiah was able to respond to God's invitation in the affirmative. Connection of this passage to the act of proclamation continued in the church's ceremonies surrounding the solemn recitation of the Gospel.

Vv. 9–10 describe the effect rather than the content of Isaiah's message. The narrative of the call was handed on not to cloak the prophet's words with an aura of divine approbation but to demonstrate that God's judgment was not contingent upon the success or failure of the prophetic mission. Comparison with the events in the life of church and believers is appropriate. The prophetic ministry in which all Christians share depends no more upon success than did Isaiah's. The juxtaposition of glorious majesty and devastating judgment in this passage creates a powerful contrast with obvious meaning. Those who refuse to respond without a display of divine presence are liable to receive one in the form of judgment.

Second Lesson: 1 Cor. 14:12b–20. In chap. 14 Paul pushes the conclusion he has been establishing in the previous chapters to its logical end. The question is the ranking of spiritual gifts on a scale of religious values. The Corinthians, being religious persons, tended to place the most apparently supernatural items at the top of their list. Paul disagreed. By his standard the most impressive miracle worked by the Spirit is the creation of the Body. From this viewpoint the criterion for value is edification of the Body (v. 12), not individual performance. The Corinthians were deeply impressed by the contrast between heavenly wisdom and earthly foolishness (see chaps. 1—4). Paul accepts this antithesis but points to the cross as the heavenly wisdom that is foolish by earthly standards—rather than, say, to discourse in the language of angels. Divine wisdom is not what people would perceive as especially shrewd or brilliant. It is what God does.

In vv. 14ff. Paul takes up another conception shared by his readers —inspiration—and proceeds to turn this upside down also. Ancients did not neglect to reflect on inspiration in psychological terms and the information it supplied regarding human identity. One solution to the question of identity was to seek the true self outside of, above and beyond the apparent self. In inspiration the human mind (Gr. *nous*) was invaded and taken over by an alien force (Gr. *pneuma*). That state was possession of one's true, heavenly identity. Paul accepts all this, at least for the sake of discussion, but ranks intelligence (*nous*) over Spirit (*pneuma*) because it is what can edify. In so doing he raises the question of whether possession of heavenly self is even useful for Christians. Reflection upon the cross shows what he had in mind. Had Christ made use of his divine power, the entire operation would have been of no effect.

The object of edification is the person described as an "outsider" by the RSV in 14:16. By this word we should understand any non-pneumatic, or non-Pentecostal. V. 20 takes up the Corinthian wisdom-mystery jargon of adult/child and perfect/uninitiated in such a way as to turn it against them. Paul says that according to their own scale of values, the Corinthian pneumatic elitists are "immature." This was one of the strongest insults in their vocabulary.

Gospel: Luke 5:1–11. Luke narrates the call of the first disciples after a period of preaching and healing (chap. 4). This is more "logical" than Mark's order. For this incident the evangelist made use of three sources. Mark 4:1–2 provided the context, Mark 1:16–20 the event, and an old resurrection appearance story fleshed out the brief story from Mark and gave it suitable coloration. For comparison with this last (hypothetical) source there is the appearance described in John 21:3–14. John 21 blended two stories: a revelation in the miraculous catch and a recognition in the context of the Eucharist. Luke will use the second of these themes in his Emmaus story, 24:13–35.

The blending of sources has left several inconsistencies for the convenience of critics. The nets were left on the beach according to v. 2, but in v. 4 they are available. Peter is addressed with imperatives in the plural ("you all") at v. 4b. These errors show us that the present scene comes from the evangelist and represents his particular concerns.

For the liturgical context it is important to note how the account resembles the call of a prophet. Peter recognizes that the orders given him come from a more than human source. He responds to a divine command, not a personal request. The claim of personal unworthiness in v. 8 is a typical feature of prophetic calls. The aura of divinity looms over this story.

By basing his recounting of the initial call upon a resurrection story Luke has achieved a vivid and dramatic setting. He did more. Projection of the attributes of the risen Lord back upon the earthly Jesus reflects a shift in christological emphasis, and other passages will demonstrate that such a shift fully accords with Luke's views. On another level it testifies to the Christian conviction that resurrection faith is the presupposition to the gospel (and the Gospels). There is also an intrinsic connection between experience of the risen Lord and missionary vocation. Both Isaiah and Luke emphasize that the result of God's revealed presence does not lead to solitary contemplation. It drives one out to share. All three readings point to mission as the consequence of supernatural revelation. Enjoyment of God's presence is not the content of Christian vocation, nor even its earthly goal. Presence leads to mission.

HOMILETICAL INTERPRETATION

First Lesson: Isa. 6:1–13. Last week we dealt with Jeremiah's call; this week Isaiah's. The theophany here should delight Hollywood's special-effects people. It has all the characteristics of a real box-office hit: the Lord sitting on his throne so magnificent that the worshiper cannot even look him in the face, seraphim standing above him, a choir of winged angels. Earthquake and incense add to the effects. And there is poor Isaiah quaking as any sensible person would. The scene overwhelms us in all its glory. Hollywood would no doubt make the most of it. But the moviemaker would likely miss the point. True, God is to be worshiped in his glory. He is all-powerful and holy. But what is happening here is the call of a prophet. Not only that—a prophet who is unworthy, sinful. Why would God call this kind of man? Would he not want a righteous man? "Woe is me! For I am lost; for I am a man of unclean lips and I dwell in the midst of a people of unclean lips . . ." says Isaiah in a quivering voice. How odd for God to choose such a man. If that is not surprising enough, he forgives him and sends him out on a mission.

This passage is often used as a rationale for the "praise, confession of sin, word of grace, response" approach to worship. Although it was probably not intended for this purpose, the themes of God's initiative and the unworthy man's response are clearly present.

Finally, the preacher cannot miss the analysis of our audience. The text is not a license to attack parishioners who seem to be deaf to the Word. Rather, its purpose is to demonstrate that your ministry is not contingent upon success, immediate or long-term. George Buttrick once said, "Any fool can fill a church." The argument here is not against evangelism but against success for the sake of success. What counts in God's view is that ministry is contingent upon the power of God to effect and bring about his mission to the world.

Second Lesson: 1 Cor. 14:12b–20. We continue here the polemic Paul has been mounting against those who would divide the church by calling themselves superior. It is clear that the problem was great in Corinth since Paul spends so much time attacking it.

His approach is clever. "So you are eager for manifestations of the Spirit? Then build up the church." That's the way you will see manifestations. He moves the emphasis from individual searching to corporate building. Here is the nature of the Spirit; it is not divisive but inclusive. If a spiritual gift is not edifying to the entire community, then one must ask whether or not it is of the Spirit. Paul spends a great deal of time arguing the importance of intelligibility in worship. True, intelligibility without mystery might lead to Gnosticism, but mystery without intelligibility is only mystifying. So Paul writes, "nevertheless, in church I would rather speak five words with my mind, in order to instruct others, than ten thousand words in a tongue." Can we not remember to love and worship the Lord with all our minds as well as our hearts and souls?

Gospel: Luke 5:1–11. How easy it is to picture people following Jesus. He always seems to be going somewhere, especially in Mark's gospel: "and immediately he went here and immediately he went there." But Luke's Gospel has him on the go, too. Great multitudes troop along behind him. Crowds throng about him. The disciples stumble after him in continual confusion, often baffled, not knowing where they are going or why they are following. A carnivallike atmosphere swirls about Jesus. For some reason people pick up and go. Peter is no exception. Peter competes with Jesus for the role of main character in this Lucan one-act play. Up to now Jesus has been the central figure. He will remain so throughout the Gospel. But for this brief moment he shares the stage with Peter. Actually he will eventually share it with other disciples, apostles, priests, and missionaries. Even we get to scramble on the stage; or as William Sloane Coffin says, we are called on by the magician to come up and take part in the act. That is the thing about Jesus. He is not a solitary deity asking for solitary followers to sit in their cells repeating mantras. He presents no soliloquy on that stage. He calls disciples to share his ministry. Here he calls Peter in a dramatic fashion. Peter shares the spotlight for a moment, and maybe we should say, for a lifetime. But there is no question who is boss. Luke's use of "Master" on Peter's lips is unique to his Gospel. It intensifies the power of the moment for Peter to call this man Master. Then there is that miraculous catch of fish. Instead of lining up to have his picture taken with the biggest one or rejoicing over the catch, Peter is awed and sees his own sin and powerlessness in a new way. Sounds like Isaiah, doesn't it? "Depart from me, for I am a sinful man." Peter, the rock of the church, sees his own inability to perform. And Jesus, who says very little, as all great men are known to do, replies, "Don't be afraid, Peter." Again Isaiah comes to mind.

It would be easy to psychologize the passage with vivid detail. Many have done so with their "I Am Peter" sermons. The stress here must be on the power of God to call us wherever we stand in our relation to him and to bring forth the fruits of his mission even though the fruits are not presently visible.

General Exposition. The shift in our Epiphany season from talking of Christ himself as a person to Christ as manifest in his followers is becoming clearer. It began last week with Jeremiah's call and progresses this week with the calls of Isaiah and Peter back to back. We should also add here Paul's account of his call in 1 Cor. 15:1–11, which is found in the lectionaries of all other communions. How is Christ manifested in the world? How does he shine in glory? By carrying on the Lord's work through us, his followers. We turn from the call of Jesus to the call of the disciples—our call. This is still Epiphany, but a further explication of what it means. With these passages (a separate sermon could be given on the 1 Cor. 14:12b–20 passage) three points emerge.

First, they tell us something about our God, about Christ. He will not carry on his mission alone. He wants people with him, side by side in the task. Why didn't God perform miracles without Moses to talk to Pharaoh? Why did Jesus need disciples if he was God? Why did he on the Mount of Olives ask them to stay and pray with him? We talk a lot about Immanuel, God with us, at Christmas time. He has broken into our lives and nothing can be the same from now on. But why not talk in Epiphany about "us with God"?—working side by side, speaking and acting in his name. The calls of Isaiah, Paul, and Peter tell us something about God.

Second, they tell us something about the kinds of people he calls: broken, frustrated, people of "unclean lips" "unfit to be apostles," "sinful men and women." If he calls these people surely he will call us. In fact, he has. A little old man on a park bench is accosted by a religious enthusiast who sports a smile and a lapel button that reads "Try God." "Have you tried God?" "No," replies the little man. "But he's tried me." Whom does Christ call? Even you and me.

Third, the passages tell us about the nature of our ministry. One common problem in the church today is a boredom which leads to depression. One would think conflict would be the number one problem. On the contrary, at least you are not bored when there is a fight in the church. Why so much boredom? Many believe that the church is not going anywhere. Nothing seems to be happening. But our texts offer us a word of hope, for the power of God is what sparks our ministry and mission, not our own poor efforts at church renewal. Maybe when we see our programs falling flat and when we are down and out, we can look up and hear these words, "Don't be afraid, I am with you," and believe in the power of God. "If God can raise the dead, dry bones of Israel he can raise a dead church." He does so through his ministry in us. Here is Christ's manifestation today: "Christ in *you* the *hope* of *glory*."

The Sixth Sunday after the Epiphany

Lutheran	Roman Catholic	Episcopal	Pres/UCC/Chr	Meth/COCU
Jer. 17:5–8	Jer. 17:5–8	Jer. 17:5–10	Jer. 17:5–8	Jer. 17:5–10
1 Cor. 15:12, 16–20	1 Cor. 15:12, 16–20	1 Cor. 15:12–20	1 Cor. 15:12–20	1 Cor. 15:12–20
Luke 6:17–26	Luke 6:17, 20–26	Luke 6:17–26	Luke 6:17–26	Luke 6:17–26

EXEGESIS

First Lesson: Jer. 17:5–10. Jer. 17:1–27 is a collection of miscellaneous material, much of which is wisdom rather than prophecy in the narrow sense. For this reason the introduction to v. 5, "Thus says the Lord," is misleading. This formula marks the material as an oracle, which it is not. The phrase is secondary and ought to be omitted by the lector, in accordance with the Greek translation, which is more original here. The passage consists of two units. Vv. 5–8 are wisdom poetry on a common theme (cf. Ps. 1:3; 52:10; Prov. 3:18; 11:30; and Sir. 24:19). The arrangement is in the pattern of blessing/ curse. The contents of vv. 9–10 are a proverb with theological interpretation attached. The use of wisdom in a prophetic context and the methods followed in this text are useful guides for the expositor in demonstrating the procedures underlying the formation of the Q sermon, which the Gospel will begin today.

Because the function of giving blessings and curses is a prerogative of the priesthood, one can observe the tendency of wisdom to absorb other spheres and usurp other domains. Everything became grist for the mills of the wise. Psalm 1 is a parallel to vv. 5–8 in both form and content. The issue to which these verses speak is the basis for self-understanding. That which is grounded in itself is rootless and will receive no nourishment. It cannot survive. The proverb behind this is not so much a critique of humanism in general as of any subjectivity that deceives itself by claiming to be objectivity.

Vv. 9–10 are related in subject. Beginning with the impossibility of human self-analysis because, as we would say, the observer is also the thing observed, the section moves on to disqualify charges raised against God. Since people cannot understand their own motives, they consistently overlook the relation between actions and their consequences. If God's judgment appears unfathomable, this speaks more of human inadequacy than divine caprice.

Second Lesson: 1 Cor. 15:12–20. Unlike chaps. 12—14, 1 Corinthians 15 is a reply to an oral report (cf. 1:11) rather than to a written question. The precise nature of the problem raised in v. 12 is not clear to us and probably was not clear to Paul. He was responding to something in the nature of a semihysterical rumor. It is highly unlikely that he was facing persons who questioned the resurrection on the basis of scientifically informed skepticism or reductionism. Of the various alternatives the most attractive is that the "progressive Pentecostals" in Corinth saw corporeal resurrection as undesirable. If getting "out of the body" (12:15) is a desideratum while on earth, possession of a body in heaven would be retrogressive. For those who are illuminated, the process of shuffling off the mortal coil need not be put off to a later moment. Death would merely have the advantage of bringing permanent liberation of the "soul" from the "body." Two general points need to be kept in mind. The first is chap. 13. In that place Paul discussed eschatology without reference to an apocalyptic scheme. The use of such a scheme in 15 is thus relativized. Secondly, the basis for his discussion is the commonly accepted creed. Paul does not try to "prove" the Resurrection of Christ in 15:1–11. He argues that the fate of Jesus will be repeated by his followers.

The creed is not an instrument for theological speculation, a source for theologians seeking a system. Its purpose is rather to challenge all Christians and imbue them with hope (vv. 12–13). One tenet of the mystery religions that Christianity shares is that the destiny of Savior and believer is ultimately identical. If Christ is placed into an isolated category, that union is dissolved. Those who believe that they can "skip" the resurrection because of their advanced standing by virtue of present union with Christ are quite wrong. They have removed themselves from the ranks of the redeemed (vv. 14–17). Denial of resurrection fractures the Body by separating those who have already died. In the language of the Apostles' Creed this view would oust the departed from their place in the "communion of saints" and thus reduce "the holy catholic church" to the status of a worldly club (vv. 18–19). V. 20 closes the section by resuming the theme of v. 12 (*inclusio*). The term "first fruits" underlines Christ's role as the initiator of a series of events that can be described as "new creation," just as fruit comes from the order of the "old" creation. By introducing an allusion to the created world, Paul has grasped a point of departure for the Adam-Christ speculation of the following paragraph. Interpretation of this lesson requires constant recognition that Paul is speaking to believers, not outsiders whom he hopes to attract by the idea of an afterlife. Articles of the creed do not exist for their own sake. The problem is not heresy in its own right but the implications of wrong belief for the life of the Body.

Gospel: Luke 6:17–26. The Gospels for this and the two following Sundays give Luke's edition of the Q sermon, here a Sermon on the Plain. Matthew 5—7 has a much longer Sermon on the Mount that has tended to gather most of the critical acclaim. Luke, however, was much more faithful to his source. He also attempted to make the passage more sermonlike in form and style. The sermon is structurally similar to the speeches of (personified) Wisdom (on which see below, under the Gospel for the Eighth Sunday after the Epiphany).

Its basis is a collection of sayings, many of which were proverbs. The subject may be described as wisdom in an apocalyptic context. Wisdom in general sought to provide information indispensable to life, to make life worth living. When apocalyptic views are introduced, the question becomes, "How shall I live now that the end is at hand?" Interpretation cannot be content to drop the apocalyptic context and come up with a general "system" of ethics, nor may it be satisfied to point to the apocalyptic element as a rationale for abandoning all that is said here. The sermon is not only "law" that accuses. It describes the life of those who believe themselves in possession of deliverance.

In 6:17–19 Luke provides an introduction for the sermon by revising Mark 3:7–12, carefully omitting the latter's distaste for public display of miraculous power. Having drawn a crowd by his wonders, Jesus will now share his message. This is not just a literary scheme. It corresponds to actual missionary techniques. Luke no doubt intended this sermon to serve as an example of Jesus' message as delivered on many occasions. The sermon is not haphazard. There seems to be a careful structure, study of which provides a clue to its meaning.

The opening section is a catalog of blessings and woes (compare the First Lesson). There are four of each, arranged in parallel fashion. The juxtaposition of macarisms to woes has the effect of offering the hearers a choice. They are the terms, so to speak, of God's contract with the human race. This list implicitly states that things are not what they seem to be. God's standards so differ from ours that the time of judgment will turn the world upside down. Present security is no cause for comfort.

The third-person form used by Matthew is more original. By transposing the Beatitudes into the second person Luke has conformed them to the style of an actual address. The initial blessing and woe speak to social groups. The following two apply to personal conditions, and the last, which is surely a Christian addition, speaks to the church. They thus represent the totality of social, physical, emotional, spiritual, and ecclesiastical possibilities. The gospel is addressed to every kind of person and has application to each situation. Isolation of a single one of these representative categories is perversion. In their present position the blessings and woes keynote the sermon by announcing that God offers salvation which affects everyone and everything.

HOMILETICAL INTERPRETATION

First Lesson: Jer. 17:5–10. Blessings and curses are odd-sounding Bible words, but they do have meanings today. *Curse* means uttering a dirty word or finding "God" or "Jesus" in something besides a prayer. "God bless you" usually does no more than accompany a sneeze. And yet the Bible tosses these words around as though all of us should understand. To preach this passage we should set up a contrast between our understanding of blessing and curse and the Bible's.

We like to talk of being blessed. In America we paint our blessedness red, white, and blue—one nation under God. Many would say the church is blessed with fine buildings and a good ministry, with people to work and preachers to preach. What about our families? Some would say they're blessed with good health, good jobs, good relationships—yes, they have their problems, husband and wife, parents and kids, but for the most part they feel blessed.

And yet we trust in humans. We almost have to, to eat and live. We depend on each other for gas and groceries, schools and hospitals. The fact is we have to trust each other to live in the world. But here's the rub. The passage from Jeremiah believes we should be cursed for trusting humans—an odd word from the Bible until you think about it. Maybe we do trust in humans too much. Maybe "cursed" in the biblical sense has some meaning. At times some today sense something missing. They feel all the symptoms of the man in Jeremiah's story who's stuck in the desert like a scrawny, prickly shrub—dried up, parched from the wilderness, stuck in hard dirt. The passage gives us these powerful images. We should employ them in preaching it. Some today feel cut off, banned, alone, anxious in time of trouble, helpless—in fact, cursed. Maybe this is what being cursed means. Not just poor people, not just the old tucked away in deadly quiet old folks' homes. Those who feel cut off today are people who thought they were blessed. Good Christians. People who believe in God and yet have trusted in humans and for some reason have forgotten about God.

Now we are ready to look at the biblical meaning of blessing. What is a real blessing? Why do Bible characters fight for it? Look at Jacob in a wrestling match with the Lord—all for a blessing. Blessing comes from trusting in the Lord. It means a new life with trials and yet the strength to handle them. Trusting in the Lord brings bless-

ing upon us, for suddenly we live with a calm confidence and security
that no matter what happens we will withstand the trial. The metaphor is clear. We are no longer lost in the wilderness—no longer lost
when crisis hits. We stand strong and tall, enriched by living waters.
It truly is a blessing to live like this.

Second Lesson: 1 Cor. 15:12–20. If it is a blessing to live with
the assurance of God's care, then it is even more of a blessing to die
with the hope of the resurrection. Here is Paul's problem: to convince
his Corinthian charismatics of the second proposition. One can almost
hear echoes of another letter to another audience: "If we live, we live
to the Lord, and if we die, we die to the Lord" (Rom. 14:8a).

Paul's problem is acute. He sounds exasperated: "Haven't we been
over this before?" Why the exasperation? Their denial of the resurrection of the dead rules out Christ's Resurrection; for the one is
contingent upon the other. Ruling out Christ's Resurrection puts him
out of a job, them out of a church, and the world out of a Savior.
Who wants to do anything as ridiculous or drastic as that?

Paul in this passage turns from his personal witness to the resurrection to the implications for our faith and the life of the church. Personal testimony (vv. 1–11) then precedes logical argument. Once he
has their attention he moves into the rhetorical tour de force, and his
logic is ruthless. Who wants to misrepresent God? Who wants to
preach a lie or find his faith a waste? Denial of resurrection leads to
all that? "Then I must rethink my ideas," says the hearer.

This passage forces us to sharpen the meaning of resurrection of
the dead and Christ's Resurrection for a secular age. Avoidance of a
Greek immortality that still lurks in the church is important. But in
the end a strong affirmation should be made for the hope offered for
all of us in Christ's Resurrection, as the apostle does in v. 20. Paul
would have us as preachers do nothing less.

Gospel: Luke 6:17–26. One should not wonder why Matthew's
Beatitudes are more quoted and more easily remembered than Luke's.
Luke's version makes people nervous. If only he could have left it at
the "blesseds." Somehow the "woes" cast a shadow across the entire
introduction of the Sermon on the Plain. Maybe we are uncomfortable
with this account because those who thought they were blessed receive
the woes from Jesus. "Woe to you that are rich . . . woe to you that
are full now . . . woe to you that laugh now . . . woe to you, when
all men speak well of you . . . ." What words to hear in a society whose

mottoes are "Grab all the gusto you can get" and "Look out for Number One." No wonder we turn our heads or squirm when these words are read or interpreted seriously. If we preachers think we are off the hook, the second and the fourth woes should keep us in line and squirming as well.

How much easier it would be to rewrite the Beatitudes: "Blessed are the prosperous. Blessed are those who are strong and proud. Blessed are those who don't know their neighbors and keep their privacy. Blessed are those who go to church and belong to at least one good club." These are the ones we know, but not the ones that Jesus hands out. No wonder he makes us uneasy. We thought we were blessed, but guess again. We turn quickly to Matthew, but we know that Luke's account is still there.

But this passage is more than a report on economic imbalance. It is more than a polemic against a lopsided value system. These are only symptoms, results of a deeper problem. The rich for Luke are those who rely on human help instead of God. Their whole trust is in man. Sounds like Psalm 1 and the Jeremiah passage. Those who are truly blessed are the ones who understand that God is the source of their blessings. No matter what else happens, God alone can be trusted. How hollow is the sound of these words, "In God we trust." If we acted as if we believed it, we might begin to understand the meaning of being blessed.

General Exposition. In today's passages we are offered a choice between blessing and curse. The choice is real. For Paul it is a life-and-death matter. We are blessed in life and in death, because of Christ's Resurrection. Christ fulfills the image from Jeremiah. We live on this side of the cross, and through him we are blessed, even though his words and deeds are a threat to our way of living and trusting. Our trust becomes complete in him, our hope fulfilled. Because of his agony on that hill stuck up on a tree, we no longer live under the curse of sin. Because of that empty tomb and the clear strong voice that we hear over our shoulders on the Emmaus road, we are blessed.

These passages converge at the point of blessing and its meaning for our lives. It is never in the instant of an overnight conversion, but in the steady growth of a humble faith. Sometimes you can recognize those who really trust, the ones who have the blessing. Not in a false radiance—that studied revivalist afterglow. No, it is much simpler than that. It may be one who has seen no crisis but understands Paul's words in Romans: "None of us lives to himself, and none of us dies to himself. If we live, we live to the Lord, and if we die, we die to the Lord; so then, whether we live or whether we die, we are the Lord's. For to this end Christ died and lived again, that he might be Lord both of the dead and of the living."

Maybe we will never completely understand how to trust or how we are blessed. But one thing is clear for us as Christians. God is the source of our blessing, the one "from whom all blessings flow."

The Seventh Sunday after the Epiphany

Lutheran	Roman Catholic	Episcopal	Pres/UCC/Chr	Meth/COCU
Gen. 45:3–8a, 15	1 Sam. 26:2, 7–9, 12–13, 22–23	Gen. 45:3–11, 21–28	1 Sam. 26:6–12	Gen. 45:3–11, 21–28
1 Cor. 15:35–38a, 42–50	1 Cor. 15:45–49	1 Cor. 15:35–38, 42–50	1 Cor. 15:42–50	1 Cor. 15:35–38, 42–50
Luke 6:27–38	Luke 6:27–38	Luke 6:27–38	Luke 6:27–36	Luke 6:27–38

EXEGESIS

First Lesson: Gen. 45:3–11, 21–28. This is a great tale of recognition with an improving moral attached. Interpretations which would deprive this passage of its value as an enjoyable story are not just ill-advised. They are incorrect. The story of Joseph narrates a fall from comfortable status to the depths of existence and a subsequent rise to nearly dizzying heights. Horatio Alger never did better. Because the lesson selected is the climax to a long story, the lector would do well to summarize Joseph's previous history in a few carefully selected phrases.

Genesis 45 includes three sections: the recogntion in vv. 1–15, Pharaoh's response in 16–20, and in 21–28 the return of the brothers home and their report to Jacob. The portion appointed excises the second of these and conveniently eliminates most of the literary problems created by the merger of two sources. On the literary level the parallelism between vv. 3–4 and 26–27 is notable. This is what makes the story so effective. A technical point is the term "fath⌐r" in v. 8, which refers to an official (Isa. 22:21). "Counselor" may be a preferable rendition, as the NEB notes suggest.

The religious theme is set out in v. 5. What humans may do for sinful reasons is not always the end. God can turn even evil action around and make it an opportunity for good. Providence involves more than watching over sparrows. In every situation there is a redemptive possibility. At the moments of greatest despair there is still opportunity to look for grace. This observation of Joseph turns an already good story into one with a religious message upon which to reflect. Perhaps the influence of the Wisdom tradition had its effect here, for edifying stories were used by parents and sages in instruction. In any case, the story interprets itself.

Second Lesson: 1 Cor. 15:35–38a, 42–50. In vv. 21ff. Paul dealt with speculative interpretation of the Adam myth by countering with some mythologizing of an apocalyptic sort, since apocalyptic provided him with a structure for saying "not yet." In 35ff. he returns to a kind of speculative wisdom that had little in common with the sort of crudely materialistic and vengeful visions of the end found in many apocalypses. The style of this passage is that of the popular sermon (diatribe). Paul's major effort is to uphold the continuity between the earthly and heavenly bodies without claiming that the heavenly body will be made up of something like earthly substance. Philosophically, the issue in question is that of the identity of the true self (on which see above, the Fifth Sunday after the Epiphany).

He opens with an analogy between nature and grace. The seed was a common image for such speculation. The seed (the essence of one's true being) can only come into light by "stripping off the flesh" and becoming "naked." For Paul this takes place literally at death, not figuratively at baptism. Planting (burial) is a necessary prelude to growth into the fullness of human potential, which cannot happen on earth. In this passage "body" means something like "form" and "flesh" is akin to "matter." Paul does not usually use these words in this way. He was taking up the terminology of another mode of thought.

Vv. 42–44 build, by means of a rhythmic repetition that is almost hypnotizing in its effect (Gr. contains the rhyme *"speiretai...egeiretai"* for what is translated "sown . . . raised"). In each case the postresurrection state contrasts favorably with the earthly. At last comes the statement that the "psychic body" dies and a "spiritual body" rises (v. 44). Paul "proves" this bold thesis by reference to Scripture. In the creation story of Genesis there was no thought of a "primal human" of nearly divine status, but such thinking was common and

had influenced Jewish speculation by Paul's time. According to the
Greek Bible the first person was a "living *psyche*" (Gen. 2:7), which,
in Greek, seemed to mean "soul." (In the original, "living being" is
the meaning.) By contrast Paul states that the second Adam is "life-
giving *pneuma*," the substance so devoutly admired by his readers.
This means that pneumatic existence applies only to the heavenly
Christ and thus will not be enjoyed by believers this side of heaven.
Paul nails this down by another point from the same verse of Genesis
describing the first person as made of earth, that is, "matter." What
is material is "psychic" and cannot rise to the level of the "pneumatic" in material form. By allusion to Gen. 5:3 Paul claims that the
"image" we bear is that of Adam. Only later will we be able to wear
the image of the Heavenly One. In sum, his thesis is, "You think you
are pneumatics, but you will not be such until after the resurrection."
The important point is that Paul is beating those with whom he dis-
agrees by making use of their own weapons. He is "playing a game"
but not indulging in frivolous activity. For persons who fancied that
spiritual gifts allowed them to enjoy resurrection life his arguments
were devastating. From this approach we may reflect that categories
and modes of thought are not the essential thing. Paul did not tell the
Corinthians to abandon wisdom. The point is not whether one uses a
system derived from other sources, including non-Christian sources,
but whether such a system becomes an addendum to the gospel instead of a means for presenting it. The former is paganism, no matter
how pious and elevating it may sound.

Gospel: Luke 6:27–38. This section deals with reciprocity and
retaliation, on conforming one's behavior to the expected reactions
of others. There are four units in this passage.

The theme of the first is "Do not retaliate" (vv. 27–30). The material is arranged on the basis of formal similarity. Vv. 27–28 contain
three commands of a single clause each. These precepts invert normal
values, everyday wisdom. In the next subsection there are also three
exhortations, each of which begins with a participle and each of which
contains an illustration (vv. 29–30). The theme of this section as a
whole is not a recommendation to passivity, which usually produces
passive-aggressiveness. One should rather point to the goal of dis-
rupting the apparently unending cycle of oppression and violence by
simply refusing to participate in it. Human misery is something like
a chain letter. One solution is to ignore the invitation to join in.

The next section comprises vv. 31–34. The theme is "Do not act only when the reaction is predictably beneficial to you." The general principle is stated positively in v. 31, which parallels v. 36 in structure. The three subsequent verses are conditions concluded by questions. They provide another set of illustrations (cf. vv. 29–30).

V. 35 concludes the first half of the sermon. It begins with three short commands that hearken back to v. 27 and serve as a summary, followed by a promise of two parts and a motive clause. The theme of this section is that reward will come from God, so that we need not base our conduct on the potential of approval by our fellows.

The fourth section returns to the theme of reciprocity (cf. 31–34). Like 31 it begins with a command complemented by an "as" clause. This is followed by four commands of identical structure, two negative and two positive, each completed by a corresponding promise (vv. 37–38a). The last two parts of v. 38 are commentary on the section, joined by the catchword "measure." The thesis of this part of the sermon is that God takes responsibility for reciprocity. Because God will take care of others and give them their due and because he will also care for us, we can take risks in relationships.

HOMILETICAL INTERPRETATION

First Lesson: Gen. 45:3–11, 21–28. The power of the story as story should not be overlooked. Maybe the preacher should just read this and sit down. It should be at least preached as story, allowing the narrative to do its work. The whole thing sounds remarkably like the prodigal son—a lost son and an excited father—but with a different twist. Don't miss the drama of the scene where Joseph recognizes and reveals. Joseph has been kicked out of a small midwestern town; the dust bowl and the depression have brought his family to their knees in real poverty. His brothers now tremble in the large office of the Secretary of Agriculture in Washington. Joseph has real power in the state. No wonder the brothers stand strangely mute. No wonder they are dismayed by his presence. Joseph could have been angry, but thank God, his theology of providence prevented recrimination. It would be easy to play with this passage too much. But the concern is not with psychological experience. The writer allows us to identify where we will. The stress in the passage is on God's breaking in, on God's hand directing the ambiguity of human sin toward an act of grace. "God sent me here, not you" is the key to the passage.

Jacob's response is almost predictable. Out of the geriatrics home he bounds with a renewed spirit ready to start packing and head for

Egypt. There is joy here—the joy of a father whose son lives though thought to be dead. So recognition, repentance, and return govern the human action in this passage. But none of it would have been possible without God's action and intervention. Certainly this narrative is a story of a happy family reunion, but it is much more. It is a story of God's mighty power that ultimately works for good no matter what the trials of the present moment.

Second Lesson: 1 Cor. 15:35–38a, 42–50. Paul has stated clearly that the Resurrection really happened (vv. 1–11). He has stressed its significance in our lives—that our hope of resurrection is contingent upon Christ's Resurrection (vv. 12–20). Now that we know that neither our faith nor our preaching is in vain, questions arise as to the nature of the resurrection. Paul's theology is rarely written in a vacuum, and this passage is no exception. Here the question is about bodies again. More body language. What kind of body will we have in resurrected life? If the resurrection is a reality, what form will it take? Our notions of immortality may not be as sophisticated as those of the Greeks of Paul's day, but they are just as wrong. If our souls live on, then trust in God's power becomes irrelevant. We trust our own immortality. Death loses its power and is no longer "the last enemy." But Paul works against this view. Death is deadly—"ashes to ashes, dust to dust." As Adam's successors we are earthly people— earthy. Returning to earth is real. "All flesh is grass." We know that to be a fact every Memorial Day. And yet because of Christ's Resurrection our risen body (whatever form) will be free from earthly dependence, from sickness, infection. Only because of the last Adam, the life-giving Spirit, are we raised to new life. The exact form of our existence is not crucial to Paul. What is crucial is that we experience new creation, not a return to some previous life or existence. So the "not-yetness" of the passage is clear. Resurrection life is not ours until death. But as Adam's descendants we can live with hints of the image of Christ because of our knowledge and faith in the hope of his Resurrection.

Gospel: Luke 6:27–38. Our Christian faith is a peculiar faith. Loving one's enemies, doing good to those who hate you, and turning the other cheek make little sense in the kind of world we live in. If management by intimidation can put one in the black in the business world, this passage must spell occupational suicide and seem foreign to many American ears. The words are not only peculiar but hard.

They judge us even as they implore us to "judge not." They are harsh in Matthew and harsh in Luke. Here "Love your enemies" can be seen in the context of Luke's Jesus, who has concern for all. The concern is not general but particular. Who are my enemies? Sure, it's easy to love Idi Amin. We never see him. But what about the ones we can name that threaten us or bring us to a boil? Maybe they live nearby or work with us.

The problem is not *that* we should love enemies but *how* to do it. Some believe that the golden rule does very nicely (v. 31). So Luke has named the problem and given the solution? Maybe not. The golden rule, like "Haste makes waste" or "A penny saved is a penny earned," is good old common sense—almost as American as the Fourth of July. The fact is, it's really Jewish first; or more properly, the positive side of a more negative Jewish formula. Either way the golden rule by itself falls short. It is not Christianity in a nutshell, as many believe. We will not deal with others rightly if left on our own. Sin is real, and appeals to our common humanity, no matter how noble, will not suffice. So how do we live what Luke has set out for us? By not forgetting who spoke these words. Only by the grace of Christ can we live as we ought. Here law turns to gospel. "Be merciful as your Father is merciful." If the emphasis is here, then our actions toward others come in response to the initiative God has taken in loving us through Jesus Christ.

General Exposition. Homecomings and family reunions seem to permeate our Bible. None of them turns out the way we think. Here is Joseph and his brothers. But think of Jacob and Esau, Moses and Pharaoh, Jesus at Nazareth, the prodigal son. They are not typically American stories with motivations or endings we would expect. None would do on "The Waltons." How ridiculous to think of hearing, "Good night, Jacob" and "Good night, Esau." Each story has a different twist, a different message. And yet, all have a common denominator. God is active in some way, whether turning bad to good or bringing liberation to the captives.

The Lucan passage would work nicely with the Joseph story here. What would have happened if Joseph had employed the golden rule the way some do or the way we might have: "Do unto others as they have done unto you." Because of God's intervention he realized the way God used his predicament for ultimate good. His revenge turned to love which turned human justice to the justice of God.

Another sermon would have to treat the Pauline passage separately to do justice to it. Here popular ideas of immortality or reincarnation could be corrected with a sound exposition of this passage. With the present American craze for body improvement, the talk of physical versus spiritual bodies could be real for our congregations.

The Eighth Sunday after the Epiphany

Lutheran	Roman Catholic	Episcopal	Pres/UCC/Chr	Meth/COCU
Jer. 7:1–7 (8–15)	Sir. 27:4–7	Jer. 7:1–7 (8–15)	Job 23:1–7	Jer. 7:1–15 or Sir. 27:4–7
1 Cor. 15:51–58	1 Cor. 15:54–58	1 Cor. 15:50–58	1 Cor. 15:54–58	1 Cor. 15:50–58
Luke 6:39–49	Luke 6:39–45	Luke 6:39–49	Luke 6:39–45	Luke 6:39–49

EXEGESIS

First Lesson: Jer. 7:1–7. This pericope opens the famous "temple sermon" of Jeremiah (7:1–15). With this 26:1–9 should be carefully studied, for it gives the parallel account of Baruch. According to that passage, the sermon was preached in about 609 B.C. There is a formal parallel in that the Gospel for today will conclude the Sermon on the Plain.

For the setting of this sermon see 26:1ff. Jeremiah stands at the entrance of the temple and preaches an unwelcome message to a festive crowd of holiday visitors. At the end he will be mobbed by hostile listeners and will bring down upon his head the wrath of the authorities. Similarity to the prophetic activity of Jesus is quite apparent and helps to profile our understanding of what Jesus was. Vv. 7:1–7 are from a secondhand report rather than Jeremiah's own recollections.

The content of his message is an exhortation, followed by a warning and a promise. Jeremiah was not an anticultic reformer. He called the people back to the original terms of the covenant, the basis for their worship of God. Divine promises are not unconditional. The danger Jeremiah combated was a tendency to view the cult, which was a means for obedience, as a guarantee in and of itself, that is, to turn the offer of grace into a blanket promise of magical protection. The triple repetition in v. 4 follows the form of religious oaths. The people thought they had God's word and were going to hold him responsible for it. Despite its negative tone, the sermon continues to hold out the possibility of forgiveness and blessing, which are available if people will cease trying to pervert them.

Second Lesson: 1 Cor. 15:51–58. The problems are: (1) How will believers inherit the kingdom of God at all? (2) What of those who have already perished? Paul thus speaks to issues which are fundamentally pastoral. He does so by speaking theologically. In technical terms the problem is that of the unity of the Body despite radical change and apparent discontinuity. By employing apocalyptic concepts and emphasizing change he completes his case for the futurity of resurrection life.

V. 51 separates Paul from most apocalyptic writers by its lack of interest in the perceptible nature of the resurrection body and his failure to reflect fondly on the gruesome punishment meted out to the wicked. The "mystery" he shares is that all bodies will be radically altered. (The plural "bodies" is possibly questionable. Paul does not make much of a case for the continuation of human individuality.) In contrast to his presentation were the various schemes of a millennium and revived earthly paradise (v. 52). Stress on change emerges in vv. 53–55, which take up once more the antitheses of vv. 42–44. As Paul used the apocalyptic idea of the "last trump" in v. 52, so in 53 he alludes to the "putting on" of a heavenly garment, the true self. He uses these notions without elaboration. They support his case for discontinuity with evidence from tradition.

The quotation in vv. 54–55 is difficult to isolate in known Scripture. Isa. 25:8 and Hos. 13:14 are the chief sources. Death, here personified, will die. Resurrection is thus not the repression of earthly existence but the abolition of death as the factor that has determined that existence. The departed live on one side of the fence and the living on another, but for both death has been defeated, granting to the departed rest and to the living grace and the possibility of new life. God's victory in Christ is the basis of unity, and so the argument can conclude only with a thanksgiving (vv. 57–58). Compare Rom. 7:7ff. The final "is not in vain" refers back to v. 14 and thus marks the end of the section begun in v. 12. The earliest, and probably the best, commentary on 1 Cor. 15:51–58 is Romans 5, especially vv. 12–21. The entire cycle of readings from 1 Corinthians during this season may be summed up in this sentence: "We are not living in heaven, but because Christ has overcome death, we can love."

Gospel: Luke 6:39–49. This concludes Luke's edition of the sermon. There are two more sections and the conclusion. The first part, vv. 39–42, treats leadership and the direction of others. The blindness of humanity makes it difficult to solve problems by ranking individuals hierarchically. This is an issue raised also in the earlier lessons from 1 Corinthians 12—14 and Jer. 17:9–10. Vv. 39–40 are proverbs, with an application attached at the end. The unit closes in vv. 41–42 with a challenge to the hearers illustrated by a metaphor. Human judgment is inadequate. Leave that to God.

The next section explains this by showing that people will expose and thereby judge themselves (vv. 43–46). The structure is similar to vv. 39–42. The basis is a series of proverbs, with conclusions derived from them in 44a and 45c. V. 46 is a challenge, worded in the form of a prophetic saying. The principles conform to traditional wisdom. Actions, not words, are what count. Through their deeds people condemn themselves.

The message of the concluding parable in its present setting is "Take your choice" (47–49). The first part of the parable is, in effect, a promise. Structurally it corresponds to the initial blessings (6:20b–23). Parallel to the woes of vv. 24–26 is the implicit threat contained in the second half of the parable. Conclusion with a promise/threat is typical of the invitations delivered by Wisdom in her speeches (Prov. 1:20–33; 8; and Sir. 24). The sermon thus represents Jesus as the representative of Wisdom on earth. The specific content of the parable refers to the basis for self-understanding. Those who rely upon the wisdom communicated by Jesus will be secure, for they put their trust in God rather than the criteria of blind and foolish people. As Jeremiah affirmed, God's promise is not an unconditional guarantee. Those who wish to rely upon divine grace must cease exercising their own prerogatives to judge and punish, reward and exonerate.

HOMILETICAL INTERPRETATION

First Lesson: Jer. 7:1–7. The temple of the Lord was a holy place in ancient Israel. Here Jeremiah stands at the gate crying out to all who enter. Imagine him at the front door of a church accosting worshipers. The message rings true in our time. Many put in their time on Sunday morning as if Christianity called for a punch-clock existence. Oh yes, hypocrites fill our pews—heads bowed mouthing pieties but ignoring the poor. But Jeremiah is not attacking worship qua worship. Prophetic preachers, or those who fancy themselves prophets, like to think that worship is a good place to attack the church. Preachers who do so either misunderstand worship or they misunderstand the prophets. Jeremiah was not a social activist who lobbied on weekdays, marched on Saturday, and slept in on Sunday. He did not attack the cult in itself but the way it was abused. He moved his audience from a holy *place* to a holy *people* theology. "Amend your ways." Don't think that you can hide in the sanctuary. Your sins are not erased by your mere presence here.

Here liturgy and ethics merge. To *lex orandi est lex credendi* ("as you pray so you believe") we must add "as you pray so also you act." If whites do not pray for blacks in intercessory prayer, how can they be expected to work in their behalf? If one truly worships, one feels compelled to act with moral responsibility. Worship is a call to obedience as one responds to God's saving love. The two great commandments apply here (Mark 12:29–31), but if the second is omitted, then the first has not been taken seriously.

God's justice is finally merciful as always. We are saved by an "if" in vv. 5–7: "*if* you truly amend your ways . . . *if* you do not oppress the alien . . . *if* you do not go after other gods . . . *then*" it is not too late for God's holy people to dwell in his "holy place."

Second Lesson: 1 Cor. 15:51–58. Today's lesson completes Paul's grand christological statement on the resurrection. There is something very personal about this doctrine, and Paul began autobiographically to put his full weight behind the argument. The whole address has been couched in the form of a reminder (v. 1) because it is not new to his hearers. There is more *didaché* than kerygma in the utterance. It is a personal matter to those who have heard—even more, it is a matter of life and death. The Resurrection of Christ should make a difference in people's lives. It did in Paul's. Look how he changed: from persecutor to propagandist for the faith.

How does he finish this personal doctrinal argument? With a mystery, a doxology, and a "therefore my brethren." The talk of "mystery" presumes that you have heard the argument in the previous passage. Preaching on it would presume that the problem Paul addressed is still a problem today. In one sense it is: life after death is a popular topic for discussion. In another sense it isn't: most today do not believe the eschaton to be upon us the way Paul's people did, *The Late Great Planet Earth* notwithstanding. The real mystery for people today would be how Paul can address death in the vocative and treat it so casually: "O death, where is thy sting?" Paul an-

nounces the power of the resurrection at work overcoming death and
giving new life even now.

Preaching on this passage should be more doxological and ethical
than argumentative. "Thanks be to God, who gives us the victory
through our Lord Jesus Christ." Here is real praise that should imbue
a sermon on this text. It should reverberate (like the *Hallelujah*
Chorus) throughout the sermon the way this passage echoes both di-
rections in the canon. But the praise does not end with an "Amen.
Let's go home." There is that "Therefore" which calls us to moral
responsibility and reminds us that because of the resurrection our
labor is never in vain.

Gospel: Luke 6:39–49. How difficult it is to imagine Jesus a
stand-up comedian in a New York nightclub. But he must have had
a sense of humor. Irony abounds in some of his speeches. It's not
exactly, "Did you hear the one about the brother with a log in his
eye?" But sometimes one gets that feeling. The joke is always directed
at the hearer, whose laugh turns to "oh . . ." And yet, here we have
more than humor. Punch line leads to precaution. Christ calls us to
put trust in God alone. The human predicament makes each of us
partially blind; so trust in each other's judgment will always fall
short. As a result, the yield of one's fruit (vv. 43–49) is contingent
upon one's trust in God. Jesus' concern is not with the quantity but
the quality of one's life—not success in money or fame, but real fruit-
fulness in one's relation to God and to others.

The challenge in v. 46 sounds strangely familiar. Jeremiah's temple
sermon comes to mind. As in Jeremiah, we have to choose. In Luke
the choice seems to be between an FHA-approved house and one that
is not. But Luke's Jesus is interested in more than sound real estate
investments. To have meaning, our lives must be built on Christ's—
a recurrent theme in Epiphany. How can we choose threat when
promise will yield new life? The only choice we have is a confident
trust in God. However, a sermon on this passage might stress the need
for this trust while offering the same open-ended choice that Christ
offers. Then the believer cannot dodge the decision.

General Exposition. The gospel is like a beautiful stone, a gem
that can't be grasped in all its brilliance with one quick glance. It
must be viewed from all sides as it turns on the axis of the liturgical
year. Can you see the slight turn we've made this season? We began
with Christ in all his bright glory and have steadily moved toward

Christ working in us and through us. We have moved from God's action in Jesus Christ to our action in response. This slight turn is seen particularly in today's passages. The ball is in our court now. God has acted. Now what will we do? Jeremiah, Paul, and Luke's Jesus all ask this common question. Will we continue to worship as if there is no world out there? Will we sing "Thanks be to God" but avoid the "therefore"? Will we call Christ "Lord, Lord" and not do what he tells us? The choice is ours. We are called to respond. But something else must be said. The turn of the gospel is not so great that the message has turned to humanism. Only with God's help are we able to respond. Only with his help are we able to act and speak in his name. That is why we ultimately trust in him and not ourselves. What else is there to do but praise his holy name and then act as if we really believe it?

The Transfiguration of Our Lord
The Last Sunday after the Epiphany

+ see previous - p.33

Lutheran	Roman Catholic	Episcopal	Pres/UCC/Chr	Meth/COCU
Deut. 34:1–12	Dan. 7:9–10, 13–14	Exod. 34:29–35	2 Sam. 5:1–4	Deut. 34:1–12
2 Cor. 4:3–6	2 Pet. 1:16–19	1 Cor. 12:27– 13:13	Col. 1:11–20	2 Cor. 4:3–6
Luke 9:28–36	Luke 9:28b–36	Luke 9:28–36	Luke 23:35–43	Luke 9:28–36

EXEGESIS

First Lesson: Deut. 34:1–12. The account here has come into being through the combination of two sources, D and P, which have rather different views. According to P, Moses died on Mount Nebo without entering the promised land because of his sins. D states that his death was for Israel and that he was buried at an unknown place in Moab (v. 6). In the present context, the center of the passage is vv. 10–12. According to this Deuteronomic panegyric Moses was a prophet like none other, who experienced the direct vision of God and was an extraordinary thaumaturge. These attributes do not remind one of a typical prophet, but they played a crucial part in later conceptions, not least the messianic. The Moses portrayed here has much in common with the Christ portrayed in the Gospels.

Second Lesson: 2 Cor. 4:3–6. 2 Cor. 3:7–18 treated critically the account of Moses' transfiguration (Exod. 34:29–35), which seems to have been for Paul's opponents the ideal model for genuine inspiration. Moses, Jesus, and the latter's disciples, Paul's opponents insisted (cf. Acts 6:15; 7:55), should be able to demonstrate their divine power and the authenticity of their message by "transfiguration" of both the text and themselves. They could "take off the veil" (2 Cor. 3:13, 15) from Scripture (probably through allegorical exegesis) and let the light of truth shine forth.

This is the context of the term "hidden" (Gr. *kekalymmenon*) in 4:3, which plays on the word "veil" (*kalymma*). According to his opponents Paul's teaching was mere "letter," unpenetrating analysis, and thus lacking in spiritual verification.

Paul rebuts these charges in a way that is quite typical for him. He insists that what his detractors call "spiritual" is mere worldliness, for it depends upon empirical criteria. The gospel cannot be subordinated to any human standards whatsoever. To achieve this polemic he resorts in vv. 1–6 to highly dualistic language. If his gospel is "hidden," so was Christ, who by worldly standards was not much of a success.

V. 4:4 is parallel to 3:13–14. In it Paul links "the God of this world" (or "era") and the lawgiver together as the agents of darkness whose pretended light prevents the revelation of Christ's true glory. By human lights, the glory of Christ is no brilliance at all, but gloom. The true glory of the countenance of Christ is not visible, not subject to verification by scientific or other empirical methods. It is perceptible only by means of the eyes of faith. Bluntly stated, this lesson and today's Gospel have diametrically opposed views. Rather than seek to reconcile them, we should allow each to testify to the diversity within Christianity from the earliest times and permit each to enrich our understanding. This Epistle reminds us that Jesus was the Christ not because he could glow but because he surrendered his life on the cross and was then raised to glory.

Gospel: Luke 9:28–36. The Transfiguration is an epiphany in which Jesus revealed his true nature as a divine being. The setting on a mountain and the metamorphosis of his body are traditional elements of a theophany. The original setting of the story is a matter for debate. It may have been a resurrection or an ascension story. Although the appearances of the risen Lord in the canonical Gospels were not determined by the idea of an epiphany, those in Acts 9:1ff. and elsewhere were. It is not clear whether 2 Pet. 1:16–18 refers to a resurrection appearance or not. An alternative is to see the transfiguration narrative as the conclusion to an early collection of miracle stories featuring Jesus as a new Moses who could work wonders on the water (calming the storm and crossing the sea) and give out wondrous supplies of food (feedings of four thousand and five thousand). Whatever the original setting was, Mark altered it fundamentally, and Mark was Luke's source. Luke has made his own contributions, the effect of which is that the Transfiguration not only looks back to the Baptism but forward to the Passion.

Following Mark's order, Luke places the Transfiguration after the confession of Peter and the first announcement of the Passion. As in Mark, this is a restricted epiphany, viewed only by a select company of three disciples. Moses and Elijah are heavenly figures whose presence with Jesus provides further testimony that he is, at least, their peer. Luke's major contribution comes in vv. 31–33a. The subject of their conversation is reported. It is the Passion. To make this even more explicit Luke borrows from Gethsemane the motif of the disciples' sleep. No blame attaches to them on this account. By this insertion the evangelist interprets the Passion as a path to glory. For Luke, as in the old hymn, "The cross shines forth with mystic glow."

V. 33b is from Mark. He had added it to make the case that one cannot rest at ease in Zion basking in the light of heaven. Earthly tents cannot be pitched in the courts of the Lord. The group must leave and move on to Jerusalem, where Peter and the others will flee and Jesus will die. The cloud is another feature of the OT theophany, used as a symbol of the divine presence. The voice not only announces who Jesus is. On this occasion it also commands obedience to his message. Luke has removed the Marcan idea of "secrecy" by shifting impetus for this action onto the disciples (Mark 9:9).

Luke's account of the Transfiguration is thus an ideal Gospel to stand at the transition from the season after Christmas and Epiphany to the beginning of Lent. By stating that it took place "eight days later" he calls the Resurrection to mind. (Saturday equals the seventh day; Sunday is thus the eighth.) When applied with an assist from 2 Corinthians 3—4, it stands as a reminder that Passion and Resurrection require one another. Heavenly glory does not eliminate the

Crucifixion. Only those who have suffered the pains of existence are entitled to wear halos. For Christians in this life Epiphany means the continued offer of promise and possibility. Refusal of the promise will lead to judgment.

HOMILETICAL INTERPRETATION

First Lesson: Deut. 34:1–12. There is no prophet like Moses. That seems to be the key to the end of Deuteronomy. The book finishes with a flourish. Imagine Moses standing on the mountain with the valley spread before him, knowing that he will soon die. Imagine the funeral scene: the weeping and mourning of the people. Imagine Joshua ordained to carry on the work Moses has begun. But we are not called to imagine such things. The writer is not concerned with Moses' or Joshua's feelings. Although passion pervades the picture, grander themes push us beyond mere emotions. The faithfulness of God acting in the death of Moses benefited the chosen people. No wonder the people believed that Moses was a prophet without equal. Taking this idea lightly or overlooking it would abate the impact of Christ's radical restructuring.

However, with this OT view of Moses, we cannot miss the comparison with Christ. In every way this passage points to the NT. But Christ goes beyond Moses—a startling fact to Jews especially. The "prophet without equal" is set beside one greater than he. Who can go beyond Moses? Only Christ, reply the NT writers. Moses saw God face to face, but in Jesus we see the human face of God. Moses saved his people, but Christ saves the world.

Second Lesson: 2 Cor. 4:3–6. Faces alive with God's grace glow with glory. Surely the face of Christ was almost a theophany in itself, "the likeness of God." How then could Paul's audience talk of a veiled gospel? How could they miss what shone before them? Only to unbelievers did Christ's light remain smothered in the shadows. Sin had dimmed their vision and turned hope to despair. Only in the dark of their sin did they live blinded to his brilliance. Have you ever tried to cover a floodlight with your bare hands? So also is it impossible to blot out the glory of God seen in the luminance of Christ. One's disbelief must be very strong. Preaching this passage, however, should not berate agnostics or atheists for their shortsightedness. Maybe our vision is impaired as well. But no matter. The *power* of God is what we preach—a power that sends a glimmer of hope into our hopeless lives. God is the one who commands, "Let there be light . . ." and the earth basks in the sun's rays. God is the one who calls Israel "light to the nations"; the one whose star singles out a stable; the one who turns dusk into daybreak. Our technology holds no candle to the power of God. Our poor power to flick on a light switch pales next to the dawn in Christ Jesus that creates new life. So what do we preach? Not ourselves, but Jesus Christ as Lord. There is no reason for the gospel to be veiled. The eyes of faith know.

Gospel: Luke 9:28–36. Moses, Elijah, and Jesus all appear on the same stage. So Jesus emerges at least equal to these two great heroes of the Jewish faith. And yet he stands out in this passage. Our concern should not be with the beauty of Christ's countenance (although important for the theophany) or with the sleepy disciples (a hint of the Mount of Olives and post-Resurrection problems of doubt) or with the mysterious voice of God (confirming his Baptism and Peter's confession). All stand as crucial pieces in the scene. But Christ is the centerpiece. To preach this passage on a subordinate point or character would be off target.

Mountaintop experiences frequently yield new insight. From Moses' mountain to Christ's the insight is rich. What begins in prayer ends in revelation and religious experience. The insight then is not only gnosis but a deeper faith. Could it be that for an instant we catch faint images of a starlit babe, a white raiment, and the early dawn of an empty tomb? Visions play funny tricks on your eyes. This one does, especially. Peering for a moment into the face of Christ gives us a glimpse of God—a glimpse that transforms our lives. After the experience, Peter, James, and John stood dumbstruck. In our silence we too find it difficult to take in all we have seen. Of course, the Lord gives us a lifetime to do so.

General Exposition. If there is no prophet like Moses, there is no savior like Christ. Here is the key to our lessons today. Christ is compared with Moses but is better than Moses. The transfiguration story makes that clear as Moses and Elijah stand with Jesus and yet point to him. Paul also attests to Christ's face aglow with glory. Last Sunday we noted the movement in Epiphany season from Christ's call to ours, from God's mission through him to God's mission through us. Now we return full circle to Christ. Again we're reminded that we preach "not ourselves but Christ." All the Epiphany passages ultimately force us in this direction. All point to him boldly as a child who thrusts a stubby finger at the ceiling when his parent asks, "And where is the light?" Whether it be Yahweh pointing from heaven, Peter from Caesarea, John down by the riverside, or Moses and Elijah on the mountain, the light they all single out is the beacon to the nations, even our Lord Christ. What better way to end the Epiphany season and to begin anew the life we are all called to live in his name.